The Joy of Six

What my six kids would rather you didn't know...

About my six decades of living, loving and laughing!

Charlene Potterbaum

Bound to Excel
Published by Bound to Excel
Elkhart, IN
www.boundtoexcel.com

ISBN 0-9763076-1-8

©2002 by Charlene Potterbaum
All rights reserved. No part of this book may be reproduced any form, except for the inclusion of brief quotations in a review, without permission in writing from the author.

Printed in the United States of America

Cover design by Mike Eberly
Layout by Alison L. King

Dedication

This book is dedicated to My Six
Children
And the Oodles of Offspring
They created
The minute my back was turned!

And to the laughin'est, most loving, Supportive
"Soul Sisters"
of the esteemed Monday night group...
(Sue Ellen, Donalyn, Mary Lou, Nicky)

But most of all, to...

My Dear Husband, Gene, who spends most of his
life shaking his head
And wondering when he will ever adjust to the
antics
Of the likes...

Of me!

There is a reason why I write...Honest!

How did I become a book writer, you ask? Well, simply by writing one word at a time and then shuffling those words into a readable paragraph; however, a more subtle reason had to do with a burning desire to finish a sentence at least once in my lifetime!

You see, as I was the youngest of five in my family of origin and the mother of six in my existing world; few of my sentences ever made it to completion. Either they were stared down, gobbled up in the middle, or finished by an elder, which drove me to a good deal of journaling, which is possibly the reason why I became...a book writer!

Having tolerated such a varied string of hilarious interrupters, I find it refreshing to have this chance to express the Love of God that lives inside of me, through the medium of words and laughter. Our world is much too serious—much too pain-filled, too materialistic—for most of us to remember how to be childlike and return to the wonder we once knew.

We are a people so engrossed with past sins and future fears we have lost the capacity to revel in each present moment, to fill it with joy and thanksgiving. We have forgotten how to get a little tipsy in the Spirit!

And how about this title! I used it innocently enough, thinking it would be a good "attention getter"—but now that I have moved into this phase of being my own publisher and put it under a new cover, I have also experienced this title as it has been garbled into the PA system of huge bookstores... and, you guessed it...it doesn't sound like—Six!

Consequently, just after the title was spoken LOUDLY in Border's, and as I was about to slink under the small table they'd provided, a burly pants-a-draggin' young man, replete with nose rings, lip rings, cleavage in the backside, goatee and tattoos up the ying-yang, threw down a few bills and said, "Sign it to 'Heather'!"

I grinned and did his bidding while thinking, Wow—Heather is in for quite a surprise!

Recently, in my Daily Word, I read that "Laughing is a wonderful therapy that strengthens my spirits. As I laugh, endorphins—my body's own natural soothing and invigorating agents—are released into my system. I feel energized—as if every cell of my body has been recharged with life. I am refreshed and enlivened. My soul is lifted through laughter....."

So that is another reason why I write. I love laughing, and when I am able to laugh at myself—well, the whole world laughs with me, usually. While writing my first book, my dear sis phoned and heard me giggling as I answered her call. She said, "What's so funny?" I said, "Oh—just laughing at something I wrote." After a long pause, she said.... "Is that healthy? I mean—you aren't supposed to laugh at your own material, are you?"

I said, "Lauraine, if it doesn't make me laugh, why would it make anyone else laugh?" And with that, I want to say that I hope this little book becomes a daily dose of laughter for you. It's like God said, "He that is of a merry heart hath a continual feast!" To which my husband replied, "Yes, dear—I've noticed that."

The Mother Inferior here, no more...

What's a nice grandmother like me doing in the middle of this Soap Opera? As if dealing with the cellulite and tug of war being waged with my exterior even as we speak isn't bad enough—I have to do deep breathing, just to stabilize my system because of the shocking decisions made by my offspring! I thought that once we got the children raised, life would get easier; but I've found it doesn't get easier—it just gets shorter!

Okay, first this exterior business. Every morning, I glance cautiously into the mirror and squeal—"E Gad—could all of this have happened just overnight? Who is this reflection that reminds me of someone I once knew? Am I even related?"

And as I make peace with this alarming image I give tribute once again to dear Erma Bombeck who said, "I have everything I had at sixteen—it's just all hanging four inches closer to the floor!"

Years ago, we often heard an idiom "just hang loose." I've discovered that, at my age, not only do things "hang loose," but they also wrinkle, ache or dimple. And do you know what happens to a double chin if you lose weight after sixty? It becomes accordion-pleated and looks like a vertical blind supporting your first-born chin.

And as you have guessed, I am "over the hill." That is a

great advantage, however, as I can't see what those darned kids are doing on the other side!

But there are assets to this aging thing. A body that moves a little slower can't get to the phone as quickly, giving the answering machine a chance to kick in so you can get a feel for what alibis you need. Most calls are from people who bear a resemblance to us wanting to borrow money, or ladders, tools, gadgets, more money, books, computers, brushes, rakes, more money, blowers, sweepers, dry goods, wet goods, cars, trucks, hoses or hair spray, and even more money, to mention a few. I have a great magnet on my 'fridge that says "Money isn't everything, but it sure keeps the kids in touch!" I'm wondering if it might not be a good idea to bury that in a drawer someplace.

However, I remind myself often that these six kids didn't ask to be born, but like my husband always says, "It seemed like the right thing to do at the time." So consequently, they were all created. Well, it's a wonder to me they even speak to us, considering they didn't ask to be here then got spanked the minute they showed up. That may have been one Small Smack for Mankind, but I'm also sure it has been one giant slap toward hostility for all generations to come! I've assured them that had I been conscious and in my right mind I would never have let that happen.

So they came, kicking and screaming, into this Land of Pick-Up and Put-Away where I have reigned for over fifty years. I suppose by rite of passage, they do have a claim to creating all the chaos necessary to further their soul's growth no matter how many times I clutch my apron to my mouth to stem the flow of parental control that wants to escape! "Live and let live" needs to hunker in a little deeper than my nerve ends if it wants to establish residency in my heart. I have a cousin who cautioned me to "keep your mouth shut and your bowels open" when the first daughter-in-law entered the arena, and for the most part, I have followed her moving suggestion.

But there is a reason why Gene comes in and throws his keys down every day and says, "Are the children still married?" I answer, "For today, I think." Then when he isn't looking, I check the answering machine and the newspaper just to be sure, because we have had so many marriages and divorces in our family, Goodwill won't even take our old wedding attire. They say it looks...too used.

Many people have written or asked, "Why are you not writing about your family anymore?" I chew my lip for a moment then mumble, "When they started doing things I couldn't put in print, I had to quit—and besides, I'd written every funny thing I could remember. And it takes a long time to build another generation with the promise of new material!" (Or, I might add, to wait until the lastest generation is old enough to have forgotten if I, God forbid, should ever repeat myself!)

I have been silent now for about twenty years. The first ten I spent feeling guilty that I wasn't spewing out great heaps of wisdom so God could keep the world more easily on course. The second ten I spent realizing that God didn't need my help as much as I thought He did and that He could have done it without me the whole time I was showing off.

But what used to be the Mother Inferior has come back to you now, in much better shape. (My Monday night group would insert "spiritually, that is...") But I feel a great need to express myself again, before...before—well, you know. There is just so much I want to say while I can still say it, before that casket lid clamps down on my prettied-up remains; and that will probably happen at about the same time they make the discovery that it was broccoli that made you fat and not hot fudge, after all. I say that, because my last child was potty-trained just twenty minutes before they invented disposable diapers and, come to think of it, the birth control pill hit the drawing board about twenty minutes after he was conceived.

As for the Land of Pick-Up and Put-away—a land my children didn't adapt to easily, as they seldom ever picked up or put away anything—(I have a niece in Australia who said that when she died she wanted her ashes spread all over her house, so "those darned kids will have to clean up after me at least once in their lives"—that she had "spent most of her life behind a Hoover—might as well spend Eternity inside of one!")

But it has been a pleasant Land. It is a land that evolved quietly, when no one was looking—stone upon stone, pop can upon ringed-tabletop, lone sock against broken chair-rung. It used to be freckled here and there with acne and nervous rashes, but the six children are now grown; the ring-topped table has been replaced, as has been the chair with the broken rung. The acne finally cleared up, but I do see people scratching now and then.

It was all atmospherically conducive to raising children, which is what I did for so many years—not necessarily what I did best, but—what I did.

As you might have guessed, I didn't accomplish this feat all by myself. I was ably assisted by Our Father Who Art in Business, one Otis Eugene Potterbaum. I have no idea how you can look down on some sweet little baby and give him a moniker like Otis, but my grandmother named my father Opces so I guess things like that do happen. When we'd had so many kids that we started running out of names, we thought Otis and Opces might be good names for twins should they appear on the scene—which is probably why

The Joy of Six! 11

they didn't. I am so glad we were able to name them all before we got to the bottom of our lists, so we never had to dub one Phillips or Magnesia.

I realize it would be much more exciting if I were to tell you that Gene and I met when he threw himself into the St. Joe River to save me for drowning. However, anyone who has known me longer than a day would tell you that my fear of water is so great that I still back into the shower and that I would never get near water that perilously deep!

No, our meeting wasn't dramatic. Gene and I met in biology class, but obviously we listened to very little the teacher had to say about the birds and the bees. We had enough trouble fighting our own hormonal battles without taking on the entire animal kingdom, who, I might add, do their own natural thing without any guilt or going to confession.

As I recall, our falling in love happened while I was having a nosebleed during class. Well, at least my falling in love happened then. Although it was fifty years ago, I remember it distinctly. But as I was saying, my nose was in real trouble. I made my way to Miss Markle's desk, head held high, to stem the scarlet flow and I snirkled, "Biss Barkle? I deed to be dis-bissed, I..." Well, biology teacher or not, I knew she felt faint at the sight of blood so I wasn't surprised when she put her hand over her mouth and made a strange little gagging sound as she nodded her head toward the nurse's office. I guided my body toward the door in this snooty (pun intended) stance. I could see only dangling pull strings and dead flies on sticky paper so it wasn't surprising that I should bump a few tables.

Gene happened to be sitting at one of these, dissecting a frog at the time. Seems he wound up castrating the poor little fellow instead, due to the sudden jar, but wonder of wonders! When he turned those heavenly blue eyes my way and screwed that handsome face into a what-a-klutz expression—I knew! I knew this was the man I was going to marry, because the Minister of my Interior told me so!

Well, that certainly gave me something to mull over while hanging my head from the edge of the sofa in the nurse's office. I mean, to think that someone with such long lashes would be kissing me every morning for the rest of my life—me, the maiden who looks like Minnie Mouse with or without mascara. Seemed to me that he wouldn't be getting much in the bargain, but maybe dimples and a good sense of humor would take up the slack.

Needless to say, I returned to class walking on air which was just as well as I'd strewn a whole lot of tissues about. And after class, he walked right up to me. I broke out in a cold sweat as I didn't think it fitting for him to propose to me right there seeing as how we barely knew each other. It would be so hammy!

Instead, he comfortingly murmured, "Aren't nosebleeds the pits? I get them all the time, too," and he walked away. Mesmerized, I thought, Think of it! He gets nosebleeds, too! We're truly compatible! It's uncanny! (I was reading Dickens at the time and tended to think in hifalutin' words.)

For the first time in my life, I looked forward to school the next day. I hoped Gene would contain himself and not come rushing up to embrace me.

I needn't have worried.

Not only did he not embrace me, but he also did not notice me, speak to me, smile at me, or acknowledge me in any way for many weeks. He looked through me, around me, beyond me, but never at me. So I went to this Something on the inside of me, now known as the Minister of my Interior, and inquired again. "You were saying?" He affirmed the same message to me and He didn't even bother to add the long sigh of exasperation that you and I would have added had we been dealing with such a clod of unbelief.

And so, taking my uncertain future into my own hands, I devised a campaign. I'd come from a strongly dysfunctional home and already at seventeen, I felt deeply responsible for anything that happened within a radius of this hemisphere anyhow, so naturally, I learned early to "fix things." As part of my campaign, I primped for hours, pampered and polished my exterior until every hair responded on command, and every pleat was perfectly aligned. (Now realize—we are talking a long time ago. This was before grunge, denim, cleavage and silicone.)

Well, I didn't give up easily.

Undaunted, I draped my plain body seductively alongside the entrance to the biology room, clinging coyly to the doorframe, planting my feet just the way I'd seen models do in the 4-H county fair. I managed to accidentally trip him once, and he mumbled, "'Scuse me," but I felt one could hardly build a relationship on that.

Yet, I persevered. In fact, I finally jumped a couple of decades ahead of the game and asked him for our first date. (As always, God's little helper...) Well, as you can see, it worked for me. As I mentioned, we have those six kids—and memories so rich, they satisfy my heart as I rock back and forth and remember, in the creaking chair that must have rocked at least to the moon and back.

Oh, there were heartaches, too, but that is what makes the tapestry of a life so beautiful—the light and dark of it, contrasting just enough to please the eye of the soul, much as the perfect blend pleases the eye of a quilter. There is great beauty in contrast. We might be able to recall a lot of things hardly worth mentioning—little things, that had they been seen differently, could have torn us apart and left us devastated. But, we have chosen not to "sweat the small stuff." And trust me—it's all small stuff—until the kids grew so big!

As an added blessing, I never had to work outside the home. This gave me ample time to think of what I would write should the time ever come. I kept notes on bits of napkins, meat wrappers, backs of receipts, McDonald's cartons—all clamped on the clip board that, over time, developed a pungency that caused the dog to eye it hungrily.

No, with a house full of that many growing bodies Gene thought it was better for me to stay there and keep the home fryers burning (clearly not a typo, for it is a known fact that "No matter where I serve my guests, it seems they like my books the best." For instance, recently Gene asked Larry to pass the gravy to him. Larry said, "Sure, Dad... one lump or two?")

However, I did work at a local soda fountain when we first met. This career was short-lived, due, I think, to the time a domineering old town sot came in, threw a quarter down on the counter and, while holding his head, demanded "Aspern!"

"Not really," I said, without flinching. "But my feet are awful tired!"

Well, that wasn't my idea of an exciting future, anyhow. All I wanted to be and do was domestic in nature. I have since found out that there isn't any one part of housework I dislike, unless it's the disturbing fact that it all has to be done at once, over and over again, continuously, relentlessly, on and on, world without end. I recently purchased a meaningful sticker for my scrapbooking that reads HOUSEWORK DONE PROPERLY WILL KILL YOU. Obviously, I haven't yet done it properly as I am still here whining about it, and I would love to give credit to whoever thought that up originally, but I have no idea who it was. My greatest fear is that it was lifted from some tombstone!

Well, I hope you have chosen to read on, and that I haven't offended or lost you somewhere in the midst of all this. I can think of no reason why you should read on, unless it is downright curiosity, for I certainly haven't done anything outstanding enough to warrant your attention—unless approaching seventy carries some clout, or maybe just because I have spent over fifty years looking into this spiritual thing and made some pleasant discoveries. I have found that being "kind" plain feels better than being unkind; I have found that moments of "bliss" were more meaningful than anything the world has to offer; I have found that temporal things didn't fill the void in my heart with satisfaction like eternal things do... and I have found that Love is the only "real thing" in spite of what some commercials might say!

And somehow, I think I was put here to share all of this, for from a child up, I have always known—and stated—that "someday I am going to write books." In fact, once I stated it publicly, but incoherently, for in my enthusiasm, I wound up stating that "from the third grade, I have always known that I was going to write books and speak before groups of large women." The immediate tittering made me aware of the public blooper that couldn't be taken back, so that is why I much prefer the writing to speaking, as "blue-penciling" is pretty hard to do when standing before a live audience!

Everything is Relative

I'd like to think these six children came about because I am so irresistible; a fact still being disputed by those same six and my mother-in-law, not to mention a few school districts, some frenzied publishers, agents, former neighbors and a few denominations.

Well, for starters, the kids have been as prolific as we were for I am now known as Grandma to twenty grandchildren and so far, four great-grandchildren. They have not yet outgrown their need for milk or their grandmother, or attention, affection, advice (only when asked for, of course, for everyone knows that unasked for advice becomes criticism and Lord knows there is way too much of that floating around in our atmosphere!) Larry, our first-born, had to bear the brunt of all our immaturities for we, of course, were going to raise perfect children, even though it had never been done before. Our children would never scream in the middle of the supermarket aisles! (Who'd ever believe that!) Our children would never throw tantrums! (See introduction to Mark.) Our children would never destroy other people's property! (See a certain mailbox we had to replace.) We would never raise our voices to our children! Check neighbors within a two block radius about this one!) Unfortunately, my imperfections kept mucking up the process, as you might have guessed, but at least Larry and I are still speaking...if I could get him to talk, that is. When he was a teen, our conversations went something like this:

"Hi, Lar. Where have you been?"

"Oh—just out."

"Have a good time?"

"Yeah, great."

"Did you do anything exciting?"

"No, not really."

Later, I would find out he'd witnessed a drive-by shooting or been first at the scene of an accident or had saved someone from drowning. His letters from boot camp were a bit more informative, however. Like this one:

"Dear Mom and Dad,

I'm so sore—five minutes ago I started to sneeze and my stomach muscles are still recoiling. Maybe I won't look any different to you when I get home, but I've done so many push-ups, I'll bet I could pick up a dime with my navel!

Today we got our M-16's. Can't shoot it yet, but I can squish cockroaches with the butt real good. As you might have guessed, I can't make my bed right, can't march right, can't peel potatoes right, but I'm still heterosexual, and in this man's Army, that's saying something! Much love from your son, Larry."

Guess he finally learned how to peel potatoes, as he and his wife, whose name is Sharleen, (who was named after her mother, Sharleen—guess only the spelling was changed to protect the innocent) had a restaurant called "Pottzie's". His two wonderful kids, Eric and Ashley, are forever trying to straighten their parents out, which always causes me to smile, for I know that payback truly is hell. And I had to mention them by name, because everyone I have ever known or is related to me wants their name in a book. I guess being listed in the telephone directory isn't quite the same heady experience as being squeezed into the middle of someone's so-called memoirs.

Two years after Larry was born, Don showed up. When they put him into my arms, I was so relieved to experience the rush of love I felt for him, for in my silliness, I feared you couldn't possibly love a second child as much as you did the first and this worried me. I found out then, the immensity of love, the unfathomable depths of love available to the mother heart. Relieved, I was able to throw myself into motherhood with nothing more than my own personal inadequacies getting in my way, knowing that should more children show up, I wouldn't have to worry about the love thing anymore.

Well, that adorable little helpless babe quickly grew to be the terror of the neighborhood, in a cute, irresistible—thank God—way, and for years, he actually thought his name was "Donnie Don't"—up until kindergarten, as I recall.

I wrote my first book when Don was somewhere in his late teens. When my first television interview came along, I certainly didn't want my children to miss it, so the night before the interview, I quietly cleared my throat and casually mentioned that "tomorrow is the big day—don't forget to watch!" Don just as thoughtfully mumbled, "Oh, yeah, that's great, Mom—but say, could you do Larry and me a big favor?"

Being the Perfected Enabler that I am, I said, "Well sure, if I can...What is it you want?"

He sheepishly replied, "Uh—could you use your maiden name? Please, Mom?"

That's when I realized how crazy he was about me. I walked away muttering, "It was the spanking—that initial spanking, I know it was!" And it was Don who sat at my kitchen counter when he was about eighteen, declaring that he was "afraid to ever get married." Well, I got this mental image of him hanging around the house until he retired, so I quickly shouted, "Why on earth would you not want to get married? And why should you be any happier than your father?"

(A Freudian slip, of course, I realized later.)

"Divorce, Mom. I am scared to death of divorce. There is so much of it happening all around." And sadly, he has had his share of them. He was sitting at the same kitchen counter many years later, watching, as his friends carried his sofa into our garage—again, due to another divorce. Regretfully, he snickered. Happy to see that he hadn't died totally on the inside, I remarked, "What's so funny?"

He commented, "Ma, my sofa. It has more miles on it than my car."

I was sharing with my sister Lauraine once that she "must have done something right," as she had three children and none of them had ever divorced. I stirred my coffee thoughtfully for another moment, and then I muttered, "Hey, wait a minute! You aren't so smart, after all!" She looked at me for an explanation. I sputtered, "Well, yes—you do have three children with no divorces—but so do I! I just happen to have three more kids who have had divorces!"

So we both did what we used to do when we were kids and the pain was intense because of the dysfunction in our home—we laughed at "what is" and knew that it wasn't the end of the world. Life would still go on, and God was still the Blessed Controller of all things.

When they placed my third born in my arms, I wept and said, "Janis—her name is Janis!" Not even knowing at the time that some authority or other had determined that Janis is a derivative that meant "gift from God." However, I don't know that her siblings saw her in quite that same light, for

Don wrote a catchy little tune when he was in college—the words to one verse went like this:

"Home for the weekend—time for a break

Good for you, but for me, a mistake!

Mark and Jamie, tearing up each room...

And Janis' chasin' both with a wooooooden spoon!

1440 is a swingin' place—full of excitement,

and as that's the case....

There's happiness and lovin' and a whole lot moooooore...

And everybody knows what the Potterbaums are fooooor..

Guess I wore her out, though, as she married when she was nineteen, had three of her own and reminded me often, that payback really was hell as she dropped her little ones off to be "baby tended" for awhile.

When Janis was three, I got her some pretty doll clothes for her birthday.

After playing with them for only a short time, she came bouncing into the kitchen and announced that she wanted to wash the doll clothes.

I said, "Oh, honey—they are still so fresh and pretty! Let's not wash them until they get all dirty and rumpled."

That seemed reasonable to her, so she decided to go outside. Within a short time, a sweaty, dirt-streaked happy face peeked in the door, with a handful of silted, grimy doll clothes clutched in her little fist. "Are they dirty enough now, Mom? I rubbed them real good into the dirt out there by the tree...I think they are dirty enough, don't you?"

I tried to explain to her that that wasn't exactly what I meant, while I struggled to stifle my laughter. I couldn't help admiring her reasoning powers, however—especially when from the kitchen window, I could hear her singing, lustily—"Sooo let the sunshine in-nn—say it with a grin-nn—mothers never lose, an-nd fathers never win, so let the—"

Yep, she's going to make it in life just fine.

I remember the day she tried her wedding dress on for her father. Naturally, I got all misty-eyed as she walked slowly from us, turning gracefully so that the train with all its lacey finery twined about her slender form. I blubbered for a minute and said, "Oh, honey! You look like...like a beautiful white—"

"Try dollar sign!" interjected her father as he sat looking over the bills for the wedding. He was going over the itemized list from the florist.

"Lanterns?" he croaked. "They are carrying lanterns? Candle-lit lanterns?"

"Yes," I said demurely through a mouthful of pins. "Flower-bedecked lanterns with candles in them, as a matter of fact," as I watched him run his finger up and down the itemized list.

"What are you looking for?" I asked.

"A flower-bedecked fire extinguisher for me to carry! Frankly, I'd feel a lot safer if Smokey the Bear was giving her away. And speaking of 'giving away'—when they say 'Who giveth this woman away?' I think I'll say, 'giveth, my foot!' and whip out all these itemized bills," but Jan and I just laughed, because we could see the twinkle in his eyes and I knew that "giving her away" was most painful for him.

After Jan was born, there were no babies in the house for five years. But the closer the time came for Jan to start school, the more I dreaded not having a little one in the house—or maybe going to work, I don't know which. Well, Gene and I can't recall as to whether he went off to war or if we just had a really bad argument that lasted for all those five years, but finally on the day after Jan went to school, they placed little Lauraine Sue in my arms. To this day, she holds it over her siblings that you guys just 'came along' but they really TRIED for me!"

It took a lot of Laurie's time and energy keeping me in line when she was a teenager. One day toward the end of her freshman year she informed me that I was supposed to prepare a dish for the Sports Banquet. On the morning of the banquet she saw me haphazardly throwing a recipe together. Out of curiosity, she leaned over my shoulder to see which recipe it was. (Much of my cooking is quite indistinguishable.) With dismay she groaned, "But, Mom! The recipe says 'let stand overnight!' You should have made this last ni-i-ight!"

I patted her arm and whispered, "Sh-hhh!" as I pointed to the 'fridge. "Don't speak so it can hear you—it's dark in there, and it will never know the difference!" She rolled her eyes and took her beautifully tanned body into the other room. As I watched her, I wondered if I had ever been that young, and I surely knew I'd never ever be that tan unless I slipped a sunlamp into the refrigerator.

(Bear with me, now. You have only two others yet to meet.) Well, Mark gets to flaunt his existence in the face of the others, as well, as we 'tried' for him, too. That gave him and Laurie a real edge when sibling rivalry was being played out. I see him now, so gentle with all his children, so compassionate—how could this possibly be the same little boy who loved to throw himself on the floor and have a good old rip-roaring tantrum when he was two? When Mark was about fifteen a pastor called from a church where I was to speak that weekend. When Mark answered, the pastor asked, "Would you happen to know a favorite song of your mother's? We thought we might incorporate it into her upcoming program."

Mark quickly responded by singing "You dee-serve a break today—at McDon-aaaald's—yes, that would be her favorite, I'm sure."

Mark and his wife, Becky, are now back doing God's work in Youth With A Mission, where they first met. While cleaning a closet one day, I came across this letter I wrote to him on his twelfth birthday:

"Dear Son,

Mark, it's so hard to say exactly what you want to say when you want someone to know how much you love them. This poor momma might be a book writer, but sometimes I just can't find the words to express what I feel inside.

First, I want you to know I love the way you are always so helpful.

But you know what I don't like? I don't like it when I get impatient with you. I don't like it when I forget you are but a boy, doing boy things. I don't like it when I snap at you because I am tired.

Mark, do keep your eyes on the Lord. Maybe you don't know exactly what that means right now, but someday you will. My prayer for you is that you will give your heart and life to Him, and that you will reach out to others in need— that you will somehow be used of God to help relieve this old world of some of its heart-ache."

Little did I know... Youth With A Mission (YWAM) sends dedicated young people all over the world, to instill in them a love for missions, people, places, but most of all, a love for Christ. They deal with street people, orphans, rape cases, and incest cases; they build homes and repair churches; they put bakeries in high hunger areas to provide free food. They even have mercy ships that go from disaster to disaster.

In the midst of this career choice, Mark and Becky have taken the time to adopt two little boys and a set of twins—two little girls who are the siblings of their first adopted boy. All of this has been accomplished with the help of their own two natural born children, Michaela and Bradley.

Now, Jamie, our youngest, was another thing. He was not thought of, never intended, at least on a conscious level—but God, Who sees all, and meets the need of every heart... He knew. In fact, if my doctor hadn't been shooting the rapids in Colorado, thus delaying my appointment by about a month, Jamie never would have arrived. I had only made the appointment because of continuing pain in my abdomen, but by the time the appointment came around, I sensed another child was on the way.

After examining me, my doctor sat back and made some notes. Then, she said, "Well, God must have really wanted this one born. If I hadn't been on vacation, and had I seen you a month ago, I would have done an immediate hysterectomy. As it stands now, we are scheduling you today, for surgery four months after the birth of this child, and during those four months, I don't want you even looking at your husband! I just think it's real interesting—I wonder what's in store for this child."

Well, I must have been marked by a treble clef when I carried this one because music, to this day, is his reason for existing. It started when he was in the high chair. He started wailing for the wooden drum sticks like Don (13 years his senior) was using and didn't stop wailing until I finally gave him two Q-tips as a kind of mini-version. This satisfied him for awhile, until he got a bit older and noticed that his didn't make as much noise. (And for that very reason, we were trying to get Donnie to switch to Q-tips!)

The Joy of Six!

Shortly thereafter, he graduated to unsharpened pencils, and wow, did that get a rise out of both grandmothers! All went well, until Don brought a huge timpani drum home. Then Jamie (now three!) started wailing for timpani sticks, so I took the two unsharpened pencils, stuck marshmallows on the ends, wrapped them with saran wrap and tied them with a twisty. The kid was happy as... as the Little Drummer Boy! But once when I was having some friends in for coffee, Jamie marched in and blurted, "Mom, could you make me some more timpani sticks? I just ate my other ones!"

Finally, when he was three, I caved. The child wanted to play the drums, so I got him a set of real drumsticks—and by the time he was four, he was playing the well-known drum solo song, "Wipe Out." There was a group of young people who lived near my sister's that had a "rock n'roll" thing going. She asked them if she could bring her nephew by to hear them play, and you know how rock and rollers love to play in front of others, so of course they said yes.

However, they were a bit agitated when she brought a four-year-old by, but reluctantly, they agreed to let him join in when they played "Wipe Out." He completely blew them away! And he is still bowling people over with his musical skills.

Well, now, you've met them all! Aren't you glad that's over? I will try to weave the rest of the grandchildren in, in small doses so you can breathe easier. It's just that life is made up of people, and people are so interesting, even if they happen to be related. I treasure the many differences, the tastes, the temperaments, the shapes, the expressions, the reactions of all these people who mean so much to me. But I also love this about the people I don't even know. I am a people lover so therefore I am a people observer. I wish that I could impress you by saying that I see beauty in everyone, for I know that God lives deep within each specimen, but I am not completely there yet so sometimes I forget. However, I am doing better than I used to do, thanks to our "adopted" son, PoChing.

PoChing happens to be our neighbor, and has been for seventeen years, but we didn't know it until Gene made his acquaintance recently at the library. They both had an interest in the Wall Street Journal and both were very pleased to let Mr. Carnegie foot the bill for the paper, so they met each other in the library almost daily. PoChing said, "I see this ver' happy man, and I wish to know him, so I talk to him, one day. He smile all time, and I tink that so good. I tink I like to know him, for I like happy persons."

They began to chat about the stock market and of the many things they had in common, so PoChing started coming by to visit. One day, I was on my way to tell Gene that "Paul" was here to see him ("Paul" is the American name PoChing uses—when asked why, he said, "mos' Americans can't remember how PoChing goes.") As I passed him he touched my arm gently. I felt incredible energy from him, as he said, "Chah-lene, you have very good character."

I laughed, "PoChing—you don't even know me. How can you say that?"

His eyes smiled with warmth as he touched his chest. "In here—I know it in here. You see, I meditate"—and with that, he put his hands together as if praying, "and I read the people's hearts from here" as he continued to tap near his heart.

That touched me deeply, and it was refreshing to discover he had an interest in spiritual things. PoChing is about the same age as our second son, and as his parents are deceased, he loves referring to us as "his parents." Orientals are trained to see the elderly as valuable, to be honored, and as having great wisdom, and he always says "I can learn much from 'mature' peoples." However, I often think of the axiom "when the student is ready, the teacher appears" for when PoChing comes, he teaches us so much. He is continually reminding me to "see the beauty in ever' persons."

You have now met the entire family. It might be advisable for you to take a coffee break now—or maybe even an aspirin or two?

They're Covered, All Right

We were homeward bound and passing through the southern part of Indiana when a quaint sign caught my eye. It read "COVERED BRIDGE" with an arrow pointing Westward, Ho.

"Oh, Gene! It can't be too far away—it would be great if the kids could see a bit of Hoosier history close-up... please?" I wheedled.

Gene stared muttering about how he spends "most of my time behind the wheel" and a few other martyr-like comments, but he rolled his eyes and headed in the direction of the arrow. We drove... and drove... and drove... through cow patties, back roads, ravines, low branches and chuckholes, to finally arrive at our destination.

I got out of the car so I could caress the worn boards that reeked with historical significance, while uttering "oo's" and "ah-h-hs" as I approached the phenomenon. But, the closer I got, the more I expressed tongue in cheek "Oh-oh's" as I discovered the bridge was covered, all right—with obscenities. I managed to continually lurch ahead of the kids, flailing myself against the wall at awkward intervals while my children, who were all able to read at this time, stomped through the relic making appreciative comments like, "Mom, what does this word mean?" as I flung myself against the opposite wall with a Mary Poppins flair.

Gene was nearly hysterical by now, and making little

snide comments like, "What shall we do for an encore—take them to a porno movie?" and "Hmm. They did a good job. They didn't misspell a thing."

We all made our way back to the car, the kids resuming a previous argument as to who, after all, should get to sit in the front seat, and that Mom really should ride in the trunk for making Dad go all this way to see that crummy old bridge! I was grateful that within ten minutes they forgot the bridge and their need for a potty and McDonald's as they were cozily asleep. Gene picked up all his orderly, businessman thoughts he'd been engrossed in previously, and I was lost in a muddled reverie of thinking how funny it is that these covered bridges always looked so much more romantic on a movie screen or on a calendar. I never once saw an obscenity on a bridge in a brochure—or muddy water, beer bottles and debris in a travelogue!

And then, being deeply philosophical the way I am, I couldn't help thinking, "Wow, that's really how life is. Things look so great from a distance, but up close they often have a taint, a burden that clings to them. You give birth to a precious and beautiful baby—it comes complete with icky-poo diapers and temper tantrums. You fall in love with someone, and then discover their imperfections shortly after the Honeymoon. You acquire a home—it has to be cleaned and repaired constantly; get a swimming pool, then find out about all the upkeep."

Every blessing carries its own particular burden with it. But if that is so, isn't it reasonable to think that, perhaps then, every burden has a hidden blessing within it someplace? I think the two always walk hand in hand. Even God agrees with me, or why else would He tell us to praise Him in "all things?" Could it be that He is working out His purposes for our lives in the midst of trials as well as in prosperity?

Could our perspective make the difference? And if one way of looking at it makes us feel better than the other way—I'd encourage you to go with the outlook that makes you "fee-eel" better!

I remember hearing a speaker say that "we need to deal with things, not as we wished they were, nor even as they should be—but as they are!" That simplifies life so much! Learn to accept the weather—as it is! It is neither bad, nor good—but it just simply "is." (Granted, there are times when the weather feels better!)

And while we are on the subject of "bridges"—I was loosely telling my friend Nicky as we were traveling the other day, that sometimes I thought God wanted to use me as a "bridge" in this book. She looked at me quizzically, as she stammered, "Like as in... people walking all over you?"

"No, you know... the institutional church and its disdain for New Age, New Thought, and the 'human potential' movement that everyone is all up in arms about...It seems to me that it all boils down to different word usages, labels, misunderstandings, and a refusal to truly investigate what the others are saying, yet they are all pointing toward the same thing—authenticity, dying to self, letting the 'light' shine through you, being mature, dropping the tentacles of the ego.

"The church says 'accept Christ—be born again' and says a lot about dying to self and living for God. New Age says 'die to the ego and live in the Spirit'—New Thought says 'Awaken to the Christ that has always been within you and drop the antics of the ego.' It seems to me like 'New Thought' is some very old thoughts being... re-thought.

"If I'm not mistaken, I think the human potential movement is saying, 'discover the hero that lives inside of you' and that is just another way of saying 'wake up to the Christ that lives within you.' They also encourage you to exchange immaturity for maturity, so isn't that just another way of saying 'die to self?'"

Nicky said, "When do you feel you started to grow into this kind of thinking?"

"When I felt it necessary to attend Al-anon. We were all affected by Dad's alcoholism, and even though he was deceased, the effects still caused problems later down the road. He was so fun-loving, and never violent, yet—his heavy drinking caused much wounding. When I stepped into Al-Anon... (For those who might not be aware, this is the organization that was formed to assist those who were damaged due to living with alcoholics. The Big Brother to Al-Anon is Alcoholics Anonymous, the branch that reaches out to the alcoholic with love and caring.) When I stepped into Al-Anon with an open mind, I made the discovery that these people were more authentic and transparent than anyone I had ever known in the institutional church, myself included!

"I also made the shocking discovery that God didn't really give a rip what you called Him—so long as you called Him! I heard references to 'Higher Power' and 'Inner Being,' yet sensed the same sweet Presence that I knew to be God! I saw miracles coming about through forgiveness, through confessions, through loving-kindness—somehow, it was more like church... than church!

"The bottom line is—we are all saying the same things that really need to be said over and over again, only we haven't felt it necessary to align our words to sounding alike."

She smiled. "Nothing like stomping around where angels fear to tread! You'd better come up with some kind of spiritual bullet-proof aura to pull this one off... but give me a 'for instance' that will make them ponder. What can you come up with?"

I took a deep breath and thought a moment; then I said, "Uh... okay, I've got one. I always dearly loved the Bible verse that says 'underneath are the everlasting arms.' But, when I heard the wonderful expression that 'the Universe is there to support you' I felt an incredible resonance inside of me that meshed the two together, and it felt so wonderful! Does that help you?"

She nodded her head encouragingly, and asked for another example. "Let's see..." I muttered. "Oh, another great one—'The Joy of the Lord is my strength.' I've always loved that, but when much younger I felt so much guilt because the Joy of the Lord was supposed to be my strength yet I felt so depressed! And then increasingly guilty, as I couldn't feel the joy, yet knew it was promised to me.

"Well, when I came across all the incredible information from quantum physics regarding 'energy' and vibrations and made the discovery that I had some responsibility in all of this, by being accountable for the thoughts I allowed myself to think... it boggled my mind! I also learned that our natural state is Joy but our conditioning by well-meaning parents and other authority figures pushed our joy into the background when they taught us fear, competition, and sent 'not good enough' messages our way, just as their parents had done before them.

"We just need to change to another thought, or see something in a different perspective, and be willing to remove the negative blocks to all this available joy!

"Oh, oh here's another one... hey, I'm on a roll here... what about 'He is the light that lighteth every man who cometh into the world!' That leaves no one out! And now, science has made the discovery, again thanks to quantum physics, that every cell is filled with light! And that there is intelligence in every cell! And that we really do have an energy field, just like the Chinese have known for eons! So, it gives credence to that wonderful verse that says 'that which is seen is temporal, but that which is unseen is Eternal!'"

My friend Nicky was getting excited now. "You mean, the unseen—like Love, Spirit, Joy, energy, vibrations, frequencies, emotions—this is the stuff that is lasting and eternal; and homes, buildings, jewels, money, stocks, clothes—these are temporal and in the same category as that which 'rusts and decays?'"

"Exactly! Only I'm not sure where emotions fall because an emotion is only a thought with a feeling attached, sometimes referred to as 'energy in motion' and you can experience a shift in your feeling by looking at something in a 'different light.' Say, for instance, you see someone in the mall, and they look at you, but seem to be looking right through you, not even bothering to speak. Your ego might react with a huffy, 'well, who do they think THEY are!' And you would feel really ticked! But, if you take a deep breath, and think, 'Wow. Something must really be on their mind, or they would have spoken, I'm sure.' And you take a moment to pray for them—well, that's a small miracle. You've extended love instead of anger, and it feel soooo much better."

As we pulled into our driveway, Nicky was giggling. I think it was because I was still talking. She laughed and said, "I think we should start a new ministry. A taxi service. I'll drive, you can exhort and we'll keep all the doors locked so no one can bolt! That way they'd have to listen!"

I laughed, too. "Oh, Nicky—I know I probably talk way

too much! I feel so smitten, because I feel like I dominate conversations, sometimes—and that isn't what I want to do! It's just that there is so much to life! So much we can't fathom, it takes a lifetime of pondering to sift through it all, to get down to the simplicity that was intended. Hey, maybe in that taxi ministry, we could have a meter for silence that went in reverse—the more I talked, the less they'd pay?"

She laughed and said, "You are one crazy person! Out you go!"

"Maybe I could be the 'Bridge over the River Why?'"

"You are impossible—get outta here!"

Now Weight Just a Minute!

I didn't get a whole lot of comfort out of the verse that says "They that trust in the Lord shall be made fat!" And I wasn't real thrilled with "Godliness with contentment is great gain" either, until I understood them in a spiritual context.

Once I asked God why He hadn't made us out of play dough so we could rearrange our physiques every morning; like when we fluff the pillows and punch them into shape instead of giving us all these funny bodies I see running around, wishing they looked like somebody else. He lovingly said, "Had I done that, you would then be spending all your time being bent-out-of-shape over this or that... and think of the problems we'd run into with revolving doors."

Every time I gain a pound, I wander through the house pinching my cheeks and muttering, "Inner beauty—focus on inner beauty—there's still time, I think." I haven't checked, but methinks I could make it into the Guinness Book of Records for having tried more weight loss programs, having done every diet, and having failed the most times. In fact, I could have flown in formation with Tinker Bell, had the lost pounds been tallied without weight gain interruptions. I know I was the only one that ever went to Weight Watchers and lost height! Yep. Lost twenty pounds, but my tummy still looked like bread dough rising when I took my girdle off. Probably because I have always said, "If you can't pour hot fudge on it, I don't want it!"

One time my granddaughter, Nikki, came running to me as I was resting on the sofa. She catapulted her little four year old body onto my tummy and proceeded to poke it for a moment. Then she squealed with delight as she cried, "Oh, Grammy—it feels just like a waterbed!"

My sis went with me when I did the Weight Watchers thing the second time. (My kids referred to it as WWII—the BIG one...) She went mostly because people kept saying, "My, you look more like your sister every day!"

We were very attentive to the slim little gal giving us the pep talk, assuring us she had lost 85 pounds, and that we could, too. As part of our instruction, she said, "Now ladies, try putting your food on a seven-inch plate instead of a big, ten-inch dinner plate and it will seem as though you have so much more."

So that was the trick! Excitedly, I waved my hand to get her attention.

"Question—yes?"

I stood up and said, "Then, you are saying that if I go out and buy a larger house, I'll look smaller in it? Oh, that would be much simpler."

My poor Sis. Frantically fanning herself, she punched me and said, "Ps-st!—Everyone is staring at us!"

"Oh, Lauraine," I whispered hoarsely. "Did I embarrass you? I didn't mean to."

"Never mind," she hissed. "Just ask her how many calories you burn during a hot flash!" as she loosened the top of her blouse.

But miraculously, every week I began to lose something. Usually it was my car keys or sunglasses, but sometimes a pound or two. In fact, my kids had it all figured out, that if I lost a pound a week, I should disappear completely in

The Joy of Six!

roughly about three years! And my niece Marcia agreed it was a great program, too. She said, "Yeah, I went and lost thirty-six dollars!"

Well, our 50th class reunion comes up in a few weeks. I'd imagine there will be quite a few who have given up and settled for inner beauty. The other day I tried on a basic black for the grand occasion, and a grandkid nearly went into hysterics. "Hey, Grandma—you can wear that next Halloween and go as a pot bellied stove!" While rolling on the floor holding his sides.

I said, "Listen, Buster—Venus De Milo was a bit thick through the middle, too, but they've sure made a big fuss over her down through the ages."

But son, Mark, parried with, "Yeah, Mom—but hadn't you ever noticed? They whacked off both arms to keep her from eating so much" but by then he had become adept at ducking pillows, so I missed him again.

But I think I have a plan. I realized that if you lost only one ounce a day, you would still lose almost two pounds a month. Heck, I could accomplish that feat just by spitting!

And, I have heard it said that you could accomplish anything you wanted to do if you only did it for fifteen minutes a day, so I thought that might be a pleasant way to diet. But in a much more tender and serious vein, I want to share this beautiful bit of journaling done by Mary Seybold, one of my dear Monday night soul sisters. We were all brought together by God, because we, Silly Things, thought we had a weight problem! But that was just a ruse that Spirit used to bring us together. At one of our many retreats (we get together at the drop of a hat—or a pound. Anything causes us to celebrate!) Mary shared this bit of written wisdom with us, and I felt it is worth tucking away in your heart. For who knows? You may forget she wrote it and will think that I am the clever one? Here's Mary's heart:

****

Body and Soul Works Retreat—February, 2002
"I am amazed to discover that the reason I am here is not weight loss—to make myself more 'acceptable' to society—or even to bond with this group (as wonderful as that is) but to uncover the Past of my early childhood. I am meant to find and relive and release the situations and experiences to which I responded by creating 'shelters' of self-protective behaviors.

"And this is what I'm discovering; that not sharing my feelings, and 'keeping secrets' felt safest. 'Hiding,' both mentally and physically, was necessary for a child who felt powerless. These behaviors became so much a part of me that I couldn't see how dysfunctional they were, and how mistaken. I became a 'people pleaser,' trying desperately to avoid the anger or disapproval of others.

"Food was reward and emotional nourishment and anesthesia. For years, I lived in quiet, hopeless despair, filling my mouth with food—and sometimes drink—choking back my strong feelings... forcing a smile or laugh when I wanted to cry and scream out.

"Now, in small starting ways, I'm revealing my Truth... using my own judgment in more situations, feeling better and stronger each time I express my own power.

"Now, I see those old ideas and behaviors for what they are. I see that I can speak up and speak out! I am free... to be me!"

BRAVO, MARY SEYBOLD!

****

But, while we are on the subject, I would like to share my list of "Beat the Sweets" suggestions. I now have five and they are:

1. Inform entire family that last two pieces of candy in dish are yours.
2. Make all cookies very small. (Guilt experienced after three small cookies just as intense as guilt experienced after three large ones.)
3. Keep personalized toothbrush and paste in every room in the house, to quickly purge any whining taste buds when you've had your little fling.
4. Carry brass keys in your pockets to fondle as brassy fingers retard hand to mouth tidbit popping.
5. Tell yourself that you are quite sure you saw a hair fall into whatever batter is tempting you.

Slices of Life

One of my granddaughters, Calley, lives in North Carolina. The first time she came here to Indiana for an extended visit by herself, she was five. I took her to our quaint Amish area in Shipshewana and she loved seeing the carriages, the little Amish schools and all the horses tied to posts at the stores, but she wasn't real thrilled with the attached aroma that went with all the quaintness.

Naturally, I didn't think her life would be complete without a trip to the local ice cream parlor, replete with old-fashioned wire back chairs and little marble- topped tables. While we were eating, the place really began to fill up. I noticed she seemed quite interested in the servers, who were Amish girls, all starched and pristine looking in their "plain clothes" and stiff white prayer caps.

Suddenly, Calley's curiosity could stand it no more. "Grandma, why are those girls wearing those coffee filters on their heads? I think they have strings tied to them."

I had to set one lady upright before she toppled to the floor from one of those little dainty chairs, as she giggled, "Did she say what I think she said?"

On the return trip when I was driving Calley back to North Carolina, she was sleeping in the back seat. I had stopped at a red light, and just as it changed to green, she sat up straight and exclaimed, "Grandma! The woman driving that car right beside us looked just like you!"

"Oh? She was really, really gorgeous, right?" I said playfully as I fluffed my hair like a starlet.

She thought a moment. "Umm...No, Grandma...She looked just like you!"

****

I have another granddaughter, Julie, who is now married to a Youth Pastor. When she was in the third grade, her teacher put a math question to the class: "Now, can anyone tell me another way of saying sixty-five?"

The whole class seemed focused on this momentous question, but no one made a move to answer. Now, I am thinking maybe the teacher was wanting someone to say "six tens and five ones" but, since no one muttered a sound, Julie timidly raised her hand, and at a nod from the teacher, she squeaked, "Over the hill?"

****

I am so indebted to something I heard on a motivational tape once. I heard a man who really cared, say "anything worth doing is WORTH DOING POORLY—until you learn to do it well!" That little bit of wisdom set me free! Because of that comment, I tackled water-color painting, and I was free to do it poorly, until one day, I did it well! It set me free to try some gardening, even though I had told myself for years that "I could never do that because I didn't know how." Well, I did it poorly, but flowers are so forgiving... yes, I did it poorly, but with love, and viola! Things began to grow and sprout all over the place! It set me free to try new things and to travel to new places—alone! I'm so grateful for these little words that set me free in so many areas.

****

Many years ago, Gene had to be in Jackson, Mississippi, for a number of months. He was a manufacturer at the time, and for business reasons, we did lots of sashaying back and forth, trying to keep some semblance of balance in our lives. On one particular journey down to see him, Mark and Jamie and I were engrossed in a book by Zig Ziglar. (Mark drove and I read the book aloud to them.)

One of the business associates Gene was dealing with was married to a soft-drawling gracious lady of the Deep South by the name of Evia Jane. She was many years older than I at the time, but she took me under her wing. One of her first challenges was the fact that I was such a fast talkin' Yankee. Softly, she drawled to me, "Dahlin', one of these days, if you will just stay down heah about two weeks, Ah'd soon have you talkin' nohhhmal!"

Another time, while we were shopping and browsing through some elegant dresses, she murmured, "Ah heah you have written some books. Ah think that is so wondehful! You know, mah baby brother writes books. But you mayn't have ever heard of him..."

Interested, I said, "Well, you never know... what is his name?" in my own peculiar northern breathless way.

She smiled in a pleasing manner and said, "Zig Ziglar... do you know of him?"

I almost fell into the dress rack!

****

Recently, while cleaning the refrigerator, I opened the vegetable drawer and when I glanced inside, I found the most beautiful orchid! I couldn't figure how it could possibly

The Joy of Six! 43

have gotten into my 'fridge, but it was breathtakingly wonderful with small ripply petals with purple veins and edges coming from a tight-budded center. I was in the process of "oo-ing" and "ahh-ing" as I put my hand under the delicacy to better support it, when my tone changed to, "Ooh, YUCK! What IS this!" as something very slimy and gooey made contact with my hand.

This lacey expression of love was attached to a very small, dead, piece of red cabbage that once struggled for existence in that dark—now dank—place. But I couldn't help marveling at it, once I'd gotten my hand washed and fumigated. I was enthralled with the fact that even in that dark, cheerless place, out of sight and so neglected, God could create such a thing of beauty. It made me realize that He works quietly in the dark of the soul, creating something lovely out of the messes we make of our lives, and it all remains under wraps until we are willing to do some spiritual housecleaning and bring it out in the open.

****

While attending a service in Myrtle Beach, South Carolina, I heard a spunky, wiry, little senior citizen delight us with her memories of being a former dancer. Her tales were obviously true; as she looked like she might erupt into cartwheels at any moment... she was so refreshing and vibrant.

I recall nothing of her escapades, but I do remember, word for word, this bit of wisdom she spewed out in her smooooth, southern drawl. "Y'know, Ah would lihk to staht a Soh-cih-it-aty, (The word is society, but in northern terms there are a few less syllables) a society foh the prevention of cr-uel-ty (add a few more syllables for her full affect...)

of human bein's, to OTHER human bein's! Wouldn't that be wondehful? I mean, people—we are MEAN to one another! Have you eveh noticed that?"

I have carried that message in my heart for years... and it has changed the way I react to people. If anyone is up for starting this "Society," count me in! We can use as many syllables as is necessary to get the job done!

****

I was telling my cousin about my first time on National TV—"Artie, I was amazed at how calm I felt just prior to stepping out before the audience. I was behind this big curtain, and then, of all things—a drum roll! But, that drum roll and the intimidating curtain pulling back unnerved me so much—well, my heart started pounding so hard, I thought my earrings were going to fall off!"

My quiet, staid, very proper Baptist type cousin looked thoughtful for a moment, then he asked, "Uh—Charlene, exactly where do you wear your earrings?"

****

Son Jamie, age six, on what must have seemed like a boring night to him, asked, "What'cha doin' Dad?"

Dad: "Oh, just catching up on some bills."

A bit later: "What'cha doin' now, Dad?"

Dad: "Well, right now I'm making out the check for church."

Jamie—after thinking about it for a moment, "Jeez! You mean Mom's got a charge account there, too?"

****

The Joy of Six!

My niece Sue was tucking her little boy, Jimmie, into bed. As she reached for the light, she heard this tiny voice say, "Mommy, please don't turn the light out."

She thought for a moment. Then, with a burst of enthusiasm, she said, "Tell you what, Jimmie—I am going to turn the light off, and then you can pretend it's still on..."

Delightedly, he said, "Oh, no Mommy—it will be lots more fun if you leave the light on, then I can play like it's off!"

Needless to say, this young man is now in a high paying job where he is a negotiator and organizer!

****

Dontcha' hate it when you are licking an envelope for snail mail, and a corner of your eye catches the "re-cycled paper" symbol? EEE-Yuk!

****

My mother-in-law, now 90, just paid her insurance for a year to save $3.50—now that's faith. I, on the other hand, had a cousin who refused to buy green bananas after age 75.

****

We were traveling home from Chicago and our grandson, Jefre, then 14, was busily ogling some scantily clad beauties that adorned the covers of matchfolders some waiters with great memories had given him. Jefre and I occupied the back seat, and Gene's mother, who was about 85 at the time, was sitting primly in the front seat. Jefre, in a burst of enthusiasm leaned forward from the backseat and blurted, "Grandma, will ya' look at this? Hey, did you ever have a shape like that?

Grandma peered through her bottom bifocals with a bit of disdain, took a long look, then parried with, "Humph... I still do!

****

Here is a great way to surprise someone you love:

Alison is a cancer survivor. Her husband wanted to do something special for her, so without his wife's knowledge, he made arrangements for Alison's dear friend, Mindy, to be flown from Michigan, to their home in Raleigh, North Carolina.

When Alison's husband made some excuse to his wife, he secretly picked Mindy up at the airport and whisked her off to a local Chili's restaurant, where the manager decked her out like one of their waitresses and quickly trained her to appear as one of the working staff. In the meantime, Alison's husband picked her and the children up and took them out to dinner—to Chili's, of course.

When Alison was seated, Mindy walked over with pad in hand and asked if she might take their order. Alison was busily fussing with the children, but she looked at her husband, and said, "Oh, doesn't her voice remind you of Mindy?" But he pretended to be intent on the menu.

When Mindy finally stepped to Allison's side, Alison looked, really looked this time, and exclaimed as she grabbed her husband's arm, "Why, she is the spitting image of Mindy! How could two people sound and look so—" And it finally dawned on her! What a reunion! What a unique way for a man to express his love for his wife! And how wonderful is that "tie that binds!" And isn't it lovely that a busy restaurant cared enough to take the time to be the backdrop for such a tender experience? Thank you, Chili's—wherever you are!

****

And here is one from PoChing: I was asking him what his family of origin was like. He wore a very tender expression as he thought about this. "I had such a wunnerful family. I was so fortunate. My Fahder never spank me, never lay his hand to me. When I do wrong, he would hand me the stick, or the switch and he would say, 'PoChing, for this deed you need punish. I will turn my back, and you must give yourself the number lashes we agree upon. I cannot bear to see you suffer, so you must do it, yourself.' I would administer the punishment to myself, then he would turn, and tears be running down his face. This make you nev', nev' want to do anyt'ing to make him feel so bad, ever again. He so wunnerful fahder. I miss my parents ver' much."

****

Once, when signing autographs, a young mother sidled up to me somewhat nervously. (This concept of anyone being nervous around me blows my children away!) She had purchased several books, so she shyly asked if I minded "signing them all?" Of course, I thought it was a great honor even to be asked to sign them, so while I was busily signing away, I heard her mutter to her friend standing beside her, that "they bring in a lot more money in a garage sale if they have been signed."

****

Although my publisher warned me that I'd be seen as a local Ann Landers after my books came out, I soon became leery of counseling with people who haven't set up their own appointments. This was due to a rude awakening I had several years ago. I was encouraged by my doctor's wife to call her friend (whom I had met once) as she was in the midst of a great marital battle, and I was told that "she really needs to talk to someone." Remember now, I cut my teeth on "fixing things," so naturally, thinking I was God's answer to the Kingdom, I dutifully followed my doctor's wife's suggestion. The conversation went something like this:

"Hello."

"Hello, Enid... this is Charlene—remember, we met recently?"

"Yes... I vaguely remember."

"Well, someone suggested that I call you, and I just wanted to say that I'd be willing to chat, if I could be of any help."

Stony silence...

"Why would I want to talk to anyone? Or to you, for that matter."

It dawned on me that I might have made a terrible mistake, but not being certain as to how I should get out of it, I blurted—"Uh, well, it was intimated—that, uh—you were having some marital difficulties, and I—Uh, I..."

There was another pause, but I thought okay, now we are tooling right along here... when I was blasted with some of the worst profanity I have ever heard! I was

The Joy of Six! 49

called everything in the book and couldn't even squeeze in a wimpy apology, so finally hung up, dragging my tail behind me, but acknowledging the wonderful lesson I had just learned—to never, ever jump in where angels have enough sense not to tread! Then and there, I made a declaration to myself, never to offer counsel where counsel wasn't sought!

Except, of course, this one time—the time the phone rang and a young mother introduced herself by saying that she had "read all my books and really felt like she knew me so well." Then, she went on to relate that the reason she was calling was because she "had a dear friend who was having marital problems" and this dear friend wanted to talk to me. Many sirens went off in my head, while I explained to her that I "had made the discovery that this isn't a good way to approach the problem," but she pleaded and implored, and finally concluded with, "she doesn't live in this area, and really couldn't even afford a long distance telephone call, and had asked me to get in touch with you to set up an appointment." That took the edge off the lurking fear, so I caved, and set a time for the appointment. She said, "Great! I will bring her myself!"

When the two young mothers came to my home, we sat and chatted and had a wonderful time—one of those times that could be described by quoting Charles Simpson who said, "If you get there the same time the Holy Spirit does, He will make you look real good!" Well, He met us there, and we were lookin' real good, but the time to say farewell drew nigh—so I reached out to hug the young mother with tears streaming down her face. Yet, when I reached for the young gal who had made the original call, I felt some restraint, so I didn't bother to hug her.

Later that week, I got a call from the "reluctant hugger."

She started her conversation with an apology... she said, "Char, can you ever forgive me? I feel so badly..."

"Whatever for?" I asked.

"Well, do you recall how you offered to hug me, and I kind of pulled back?"

"Yes," I said, "But I didn't think anything of it—not everyone is as demonstrative as I am, so it wasn't a problem at all. So, I don't know why you are offering an apology..."

"Well, see—I had read all your books, and felt like I loved you so much, even though we had never met—but when you greeted us at the door, my heart did a flip, because you—well, I hardly know how to say this, but you looked exactly like the woman my father deserted my mother for!... And my thoughts were reeling! Charlene, I kid you not—your eyes, your dimples, your glasses, your hair—even the sound of your voice—everything! You looked exactly like her—and I never could see what my father ever saw in her!"

She continued to prattle on, but finally realized I was stifling great guffaws that wanted to escape, so she retraced her conversation in her head—and wound up being totally embarrassed for having expressed herself in such a way. I assured her that it was fine and would probably wind up being in a book someday as I felt it was so rich, it needed to be shared. I assured her that life was much more fun when you were willing to laugh at yourself and lighten up and not take things too seriously.

Wonderment

Everything I have written prior was written before the day we will never forget—that day when the sky was balmy blue and the air was crisp with the promise of a gorgeous September Day, and school children had nothing to fear, other than study hall shootings and strangers lurking in shadows, and how to say "No" to drugs.

Then, truly 'out of the blue'—our lives were paralyzed by terrorist zealots who were trained to fly our planes and flew them right into one of the finest symbols of working together we had come up with yet—the Twin Towers of the World Trade Center. Numb and stricken, we watched as we saw the replays, over and over again... watched so much and so often, we were warned to stay away from our TV's lest depression overtake us and illness set in.

It wasn't too long until a thin, frightening ribbon of yellow ticked by on the bottom of our TV, notifying us of the names of those who had been killed. Through my tears, one name in particular stuck in my mind. I said her name often, wondering "Nicosia... I wonder how that is pronounced... Nicosia..."

Little did I know at the time that it was the married name of the curly-headed darling I had met when she was about three or four, just prior to her family moving from this area. (Kathy Nicosia was a flight attendant aboard the plane that struck the first tower, AA flight #11.)

Her mother, Phyllis, was my sister's good friend when we were all growing up together. Phyllis' sister, Janet, and I spent much of our time hiding and snickering, as the two older sisters plotted to send us to a different planet but allowed a different room to suffice for the moment. I remember the nostalgia of the chocolate fudge sessions—fudge so runny, it had to be eaten with a spoon, and the popcorn and apples that went so well with it all. I remember the playhouse and the hollyhock dolls, the tennis sessions... and the smell of summer that was everywhere in those days.

Then, the big sisters had the audacity to grow up and marry, of all things! Next, babies stared coming along, as years ago we did it in that order. But, also, family career shifts came, too, so vast periods of time and distance slipped wedges into our togetherness. Yet, as the reality of deaths and losses came along, we saw each other momentarily— but always with the promise that we would make plans to meet in the midst of happier circumstances and talk about old loves and new fears

But time, that most elusive essence, kept getting lost in the folds of our dramas and we never got together again until—9/11! So, once again, we were huddled tearfully in the midst of another tragic trauma. We went to Kathy's Memorial Service, and there we vowed—again—that we would meet in the future in some happy circumstance and that surely we could make this happen.

As a memorial to Kathy, and because God has such a gentle way of touching many through the words of others, I want to share the letter I wrote to her heart-broken mother.

"My dear Phyllis,

I wanted so much to call you after I heard of your tragic loss, but had no current phone number. Then I remembered that sometimes, a written note can be even more comforting.

The Joy of Six! 53

Not that what I am going to say will be all that profound—but hopefully oodles of Love will come wafting your way when you open this letter, as that would be what Lauraine and I are hoping for. Because another name for God is Love, and our desire is that He will surround you, infuse you, touch you and fill you—with Himself, in the shape of Love that comes from all those who are so affected by your loss.

Phyllis, in the midst of these tragic events, can you feel the tenderness, the caring? They express the goodness that God extends to all of us right now. Hearts are being searched—people are turning to one another—we are taking our thoughts off material things and getting to those more important issues. And please know that God did not 'take' your daughter—her death was caused by those who still live under the intrigue of man's inhumanity to man. Nothing will be accomplished if we fill our hearts with hatred toward these people.

I am giving you a difficult assignment, but I ask you to do this for Kathy. Remember that what she endured, she only had to endure it that one time. If you replay it in your mind, over and over... that is like her having to endure it again and again because it becomes a torturous exercise for you, causing you increasing pain. Phyllis, you are the only thinker in your mind—Jesus asks us to 'take each thought captive and bring it to the obedience of Christ.' I think that means that when the disastrous thoughts come your way, you must take an imaginary 'ice tong' and put the thought aside, by replacing it with some vibrant thought or memory of Kathy that fills you with delight and love. Do this in memory of her and the grief will someday dissipate... but in the meantime, cry as much as you need to—and love much.

I love you—Char Potterbaum"

A short time later, an article appeared in the Time magazine with a picture of Phyllis' son, Dr. Larry Hawk, (brother to Kathy Nicosia), a veterinarian and head of the National Society for the Prevention of Cruelty to Animals. His time of mourning was spent serving, as he headed up the teams at Ground Zero—teams who aided valuable search animals, protecting their feet with special 'booties' as they sniffed through the rubble, and returned animals to their owners as they were found. Can you imagine his feelings as he did this? Knowing that that pile of rubble contained the remains of his sister?

But those who died did not die in vain. Their deaths created a moving tidal wave of compassion, tenderness, of togetherness... and we will never again be the same. And, so—is it possible for us to slip back into that joyful mode we had going? I think so, because life is sweet as well as bitter, flexible, tough as well as tender, but most of all—it can be hilariously, therapeutically, laughable!

So, to the dear souls who have experienced such poignant losses, allow not only our love but our humor, as well, to wipe away the tears. Your loved ones who have left this domain would want you to rejoice in life, even as you rejoice in their sweet memories. They know that for you— Life is for the living! And a fulfilling lifestyle includes laughter!

And so... On with the Show!

Allow me to share one of the most embarrassing, hilarious, rip-roaring fiascoes we ever created, even without knowing we were creating it! This little incident happened many years ago while all the offspring hadn't yet—sprung off, I mean, but were still living at our address. Enjoy!

Now, I Lay Me Down To Sleep

I stifled a yawn as I stuffed the choir music into its thumb-worn folder. Practice was over, and I couldn't wait to get into my own rumpled bed where my very own rumpled husband would be waiting for me. It had been a long day. My pre-schoolers were recovering form the mumps and their peevishness indicated they were recovering satisfactorily. For two weeks, now, I'd felt like a lost gnome wallowing around in the Land of Pick-up and Put-away.

I smiled as I recalled the parting shot to my husband as I was going out the door—"Honey, don't leave the house unattended. If a thief came in and ransacked, we'd have no way of knowing he'd ever been here!"

But the kids were making such an uproar I doubt he even heard me. The older ones were doing homework in various parts of the house, so the loaded hint was lost on them.

You see, it isn't that I don't like housework. It's just that it all has to be so everlastingly done and seemingly all done at the same time. That's what gets to me. And having the six kids wasn't the problem. It's just that they had to be so everlastingly raised all at the same time, and seemingly, six kids and a clean house were so incompatible. That's what gets to me.

Oh, well. There was always tomorrow for tidying. Tonight was for resting and the thought of it made my eyelids heavy and my heart light.

Hoping to avoid some of the after-(choir) glow chatter, I quietly eased my way to the back of the sanctuary. While I was congratulating myself on what appeared to be a smooth getaway, the pastor caught my arm. "Char, I'm in a real bind. Could you help me... please?"

I wasn't feeling a bit like Mother Teresa, but I heard myself muttering something that sounded like... "Oh, well—sure, I'll help—If I can, uh... Yeah, sure... What's up?"

Nervously, he ran his fingers through his hair. "We have a lady missionary in town. She wasn't supposed to be here until the weekend. I have no place to put her up for the night—thought about you having such a big house, and all—could you possibly?"

Slowly, I sank into the last pew.

Now, I've already told you my house was not missionary clean, which, to my way of thinking was just a notch or so below mother-in-law-clean. I'd daresay my house was barely above keep-the-authorities-off-my-back clean. Yet, I heard from what seemed like a far distance, some deluded idiot chirping, "Sure, I can do that. Just take your time bringing her over. Does she appear to be, uh, easy going?"

"Well, I haven't met her yet, but the Mission Director told me she was young, serious, devout and very work-oriented." *And she's going to spend a night in the trauma center? What better training could she get?* My thoughts screeched on as I bade him goodbye.

He watched me, waving, as I made my way to the car. I wanted to look cool and all-together, but the minute he was out of my sight, I sped like a bat out of—of the tattered hymnal, burst through the door and started cramming bits of strewn debris into any available baskets, closets,

The Joy of Six!

drawers or piano benches within arm's reach. Incoherently, I explained the situation to Gene, my dear husband, who'd long ago become quite adept at decoding my hysteria.

He merely rolled his eyes in mock disbelief as he folded his paper and joined in the foray, muttering, "Only *you* would invite Mary Poppins in for a midnight snack!"

In true Dick Van Dyke style, he armed himself with a functional stool-brush and pip-pipped his way mincingly into the bathroom. He gave a little whistle and set to work, grinning. I earnestly hoped she wouldn't mind sharing the only bath with the entire family, but then again, I told myself, *she's here for missionary training. She should be glad it's inside and flushes!*

Besides, a bed would be her greatest concern. *Good heavens, a bed!*

Hurriedly, I made my way to the second floor, took one peek at the spare bedroom and leaned weakly against the door. No amount of charging adrenalin could whisk away the train tracks, leftover PBJ, Legos and general clutter a-la preschooler, for that room was loosely called a playroom, as well.

Our room! Of course! I'll change the sheets, fluff the pillows, turn the lights low and hide the ironing! That will work! Then Gene and I can sleep in the spare room! Our room had been recently decorated and rearranged so the latest batch of crayon marks on the chest now faced the wall, and the toddler who loved to peel off loose wallpaper hadn't made it that far up the stairs, yet.

So I stepped to the next room and prayed for a miracle. After a few moments of fluffing, shuffling, and the spreading of wind-whipped sheets, a fresh-spring fragrance filtered throughout the upstairs. *Yep, this'll do just fine.*

Also, I'd made cookies that day. The smell of coffee,

fresh sheets, and home-made goodies would give me some domestic credibility in her eyes. It seemed like a pretty good scheme, but Gene's assignment in the bathroom must have been tougher than mine, because I sensed the reeking ammonia might overpower the wind-blown sheets.

I hurried down the stairs, hoping to sit a moment before their arrival, but on the bottom step I heard the insistent jangle of the doorbell. I sauntered to the door, wanting to appear calm and efficient—but the little hair line of perspiration on my forehead gave me away.

Gene was still in the bathroom, so the pastor introduced the two of us quickly then offered to take her luggage upstairs. "Just put it in the room with the open door," I purred. "The kids are fast asleep." (I wasn't about to have anyone peeking into the spare room!)

By the time Gene emerged from the gleaming interior of the reeking bathroom I remembered why the coffee hadn't overpowered the ammonia. I'd forgotten to make it, so I invited Mary Poppins into the kitchen, hoping to put her at ease.

"Tell me a bit about yourself," I prattled as I clumsily dropped the coffee grounds, missing the strainer by inches. "How do they prepare you for the jungles?" I nervously twittered as I swiped at the coffee grounds, pushing most of them to the floor.

"Well," she muttered as she used her thumbnail to remove a chunk of dried cereal from my table top, "We missionary nurses are trained to be prepared for anything. War, famine, floods—just about anything."

Inwardly, I wondered how those catastrophes compared on a scale from one to ten with raising six children. "Well, if my children were all up and running, you'd think you were still in training. I've often thought that going to the

The Joy of Six!

mission field might be easier than raising six kids—heh, heh... well, probably not," I added as she remained a bit humorless over this last comment.

"By the way," I said as I poured coffee into cups that hadn't seemed that chipped before, "I hope you enjoy children, as they will be swarming all over the house in the morning. And don't be surprised if one gets in bed with you, as I'm giving you our bedroom."

"Oh," she cried. "I don't mean to put you out this way! I didn't mean to take your bed!" I assured her it wasn't a problem, and she assured me that yes, she loved, really *loved* children! As I made my way into the living room with my tray of refreshments to join the men I wondered which of the two of us was the biggest liar.

The two men were settling world affairs as only men can, when someone mentioned last Sunday's fiasco. You see, my toddler had broken ranks with the nursery crew and had waddled up the stairs with his pants at half-mast, ran down the center aisle and jumped into my lap in the choir loft, hollering boisterously, "I can't get my pants zipped!" But the pastor's only comment about the incident was, "My, I can't believe how big those kids are getting."

By now, it was really getting late and my eyes looked like glazed doughnuts, probably because I'd eaten two for breakfast, as guilt has a way of doing that to me. I was vastly relieved to hear the pastor say that he needed to get going, because I inwardly agreed with him, heartily.

Gene said, "Oh, Miss Popp—er, Miss Reynold's luggage—I'll get it."

Pastor said, "I've already taken care of it, Gene. Char told me where to put it—have a good night, all of you!" and quickly, he was gone.

Finally relieved of his social obligations, Gene returned

to his newspaper. Throwing a before-I-was-so-rudely-interrupted look my way, he asked if we'd mind if he *finished* reading his newspaper, and would we excuse him, please? We assured him that we were ready to retire, and told him goodnight—in two or three languages, as I recall.

I took her to our bedroom, made her acquainted with the lights, told her the closet door was broken so she wouldn't open it, and then we said goodnight—in two or three languages as I recall. I made my way to the spare room, and sighed rapturously as I sank into the lumpy confines of the bed. But it seemed—Oh, well. Whatever I'd forgotten to do, I'd remember tomorrow. Sleep seemed so appealing.

I remembered the "forgotten something" when I heard the voice of my quaking husband, hissing, which is about what a shout sounds like when you don't want to be heard by the party in the next room, but you have a need to shout... "Charlene Potterbaum! Have you lost your mind, woman! I'll never forgive you! I just went to the bed I am accustomed to going to and wound up with Mary Poppins! You didn't even tell me—explain yourself!"

I choked back a fit of giggles by cramming the sheet into my mouth as he continued. "Char—will you stop snickering and listen? This is no laughing matter! Char, get a hold of yourself!"

"Oh, Gene—I am so sorry! I thought I—well, I guess it just slipped my mind, I was so tired!" I was laughing hysterically now, and the tears were flowing down my face. I tried desperately to take his plight as seriously as he did, but somehow, it just all made me howl the more.

And then *he* started to get tickled. Some of his anger was deflected by my giggling, and soon he was laughing, too, but his voice still shook with emotion. "Now, stop that—and listen to me! I'm supposed to introduce her to

The Joy of Six! 61

the Sunday school class—and I can't bear to face her, I'm so embarrassed! What am I going to do?"

"Well, you could start by introducing her as your 'warm, intimate friend.'"

He groaned. "But, you know what saved my life? She had both pillows. If I hadn't hunted all over for my pillow, she might not have awakened, and that would have been even harder to explain to her mission board, because I truly thought I was in bed with you..." His voice trailed off.

Lovingly, I put my arm around him—in kind of a half-nelson, as I recall. "It's okay, honey. Go to sleep. If she looks radiant in the morning, you'll have some explaining to do. But for the moment—just go to sleep—here—with me."

And then I laid us both down to sleep, praying the Lord his soul to keep... not to mention his reputation.

The next morning, Gene took off at the crack of dawn. I wasn't too sure what one should say to a missionary who had been in bed with your husband, so after making some lame conversation and a rather weak stab at apologizing, she brushed it all aside by spluttering, "Oh, don't give it a second thought! We missionary nurses are trained to be prepared for anything! But, I do remember thinking, 'My, her children *are* big!'"

Having Tea with PoChing

PoChing popped in yesterday about noon. When I saw his friendly face at the front door, he said, "I would be ver' pleased to have you and Gene come lunch with me."

I said, "PoChing, Gene isn't here—and look at me!" I was in gardening clothes and drying my hair "naturally" which gave me a bit of an unkempt look. However, he was used to finding me like this, because he is always guided by the philosophy he calls "unexpectedly," and when people drop in on you "unexpectedly" they have to take you as you are.

"Well, come in and we'll have one of those awful cups of American tea I'm always trying to improve on..." He smiled and stepped inside, and I knew that even should I come up with some really rotten tasting tea, he would accept it graciously, with reverence and thanksgiving. However, I have come to love his philosophy of "unexpectedly" because he always seemed to show up when I needed him. I was really feeling fussed up about someone's disturbing habit of procrastination, so the first thing he said was, "Well, Chauh-lene, are you feeling harmony in your heart today?" as he pulled out a chair in the kitchen.

Oops—busted! I thought, as I marveled at his sensitivity. He was an attentive listener as he allowed me to "dump" my current feelings on him, and he looked thoughtful as I sputtered on with vigor and brought up some other peevish concerns while I was at it.

"Ah, Chah-lene—some days, our heart like a puppy..."

"Uh, do you mean 'puppy?' Or do you mean 'poppy?'"

"Yes... you know, puppy—just like I said, puppy so fragile flower—so easy to bruise, easy to droop. But one must train heart be like elephant!"

"Elephant?" I laughed.

"Yes, like elephant... he got thick skin, plod along, putting jes' one foot down at time, and then the udder foot... he have small boys follow him, get at him with sticks, he jes' pay them no mind—never faze him at all... he go along, swing trunk happy way, nutting bodder him... he notice only what front of him... plod along, plod along. He nev' boddered by what udders do, or don't do."

That gave my 'poppy' heart something to strengthen it, and I hoped his analogy hadn't been inspired by my suit of flesh having a rather checked look, much like elephant hide from 'hanging' around for these six decades!

A little later, we were talking about different things in his culture as compared to ours. He said, "In our culture, we have no word for 'love.' We nev' say 'I love you.' And we have no word for marriage, either."

I squealed, "PoChing! Then how did you ever ask Sue to be your wife? How did you ever accomplish that?" He got all embarrassed as he thought about it and laughingly tried to put it into intelligible words.

"Well," he said, "we would say 'will you take my hand for the long journey' and the lady would know what you mean. My great-great-grandfather was very poetic when he asked his many wives to marry him."

He smiled when he saw my expression, for it must have said and-how-many-would-that-be? He explained that in Taiwan, there were thirteen harbors; so of course, his grandfather needed thirteen wives to take care of each shop. He explained that a hundred and fifty years ago, this was a normal thing. When I asked him which grandmother his line came from, he said, "Number seven." PoChing spoke lovingly as he reminisced. "He have great artistic talent, both for writing and expressing himself from deep place inside. He would make beautiful fan for the ladies, and he would inscribe them with great flourishes from his talented hands. If gentle womens not so highly educated, he always know how to approach them ver' simply. If approaching new wife, and know she have deepness to unner'stan what he saying, he would write 'tonight, when moon shining brightly, I wish that your shoes be beside my shoes.' Once, I saw fan he did that say a 'lovely frog jump into ancient pond, ker-plop, making many ripples. Just so is my heart disturbed by you.'"

He tugged at his chin a bit then said, "I have notice in your culture, word 'love' has a ver' small voice. People say 'I love you for all time' at altar, then one small mistake and poof—all over, big divorce be on way! But in our culture, what heart express as 'love'—tenderness, kindnesses, sensing what other need—that have Big Voice, come from deep place inside of you. However, sometimes Chinese men not so nice to wife; but always nice to chil'runs...always, they have soft place in heart for the chil'runs—yes."

I always find myself so much more at peace after PoChing and I have had a chance to share; he mentions the "flow" of life and how things that happened last week or last year are now just a memory, and "ver' soon, that which bodder you today, will become memory, too—and you fohget what bodder you, for it is all like a dream...only what you tink about in present moment really matter. Yes, what you tink, and how you feel. Want peace for udders? Feel peace in

The Joy of Six!

own heart. Want love from udders? Give love to own self, first, then not notice whedder udders love you or not...you too busy feeling Love from God inside you to notice lack of any kind. Ummm, yes. That way to have happy life."

PoChing and I have a feeling of kinship, because we love deeply the same God. Very early in our friendship, we established that we both had a profound love for the same Creator of the Universe, though we might put a different name to Him. PoChing says, "Really, Chah-lene—in truth, He is the God of the No-Name—the Jeh-hov-a-God, and early Jew peoples nev' even say His Name—too holy, That Name. But we comes along, always want name for ever'ting, so God say—okay. One Name—I AM. Anudder Name be Love...'nudder Name be God, Holy Spirit, Jesus, the Christ...but all the same Energy—all be that Life Force inside us, beating our hearts, breathing our lungs, sending wonnerful ideas into our busy minds. He be that same Energy that fills the heaven and the earth, and makes a baby coo and little birdie to sing. He be that same Energy make our heart sing when we get in good vibration with good health and well-being! He all 'round us, inside us, closer even than breathing, this wonnerful God—yes, He is...Ummm, yes."

If he senses that I have moved into a blaming groove, he gently reminds me that Jesus taught us to "love your neighbor as yourself." He will say, "Chah-lene—if Jesus say you to love your neighbor as yourself, then you ARE that neighbor---you are one! He mean for you to see that you—would not hurt you—so it become ver'simple forgive udder person—jus' tink of him having bad day, and go on way in happiness—Okay, Chah-lene? You unner'stan', yes?"

After our conversation, I said, "PoChing—shall we set a

date for lunch, then?"

He grinned mischievously, as he said, "Ah, no—always 'unexpectedly'! I come to door, if you, Gene can go—we go. Never mind setting time. Right time will come when we go, udderwise—everything fine as is...we wait 'til time is right, okay?"

And that quickly he was gone. The bible talks about "not forgetting to entertain strangers, because some have entertained angels unawares." It wouldn't take much to make me think PoChing came from another realm, except I know he lives in a home one block down the street, has a wife and two children and a great sense of humor.

Vickey Victorious!

Many years ago, I got a phone call from Gene's cousin, Vickey. She and I didn't know each other too well, but we'd always had delightful times together at family reunions and baby showers, and even managed a giggle or two during funerals when no one was listening.

At the time Vickey called me, I was working on my first book while fighting a flu bug, wrapped in an afghan surrounded by inhalers, vapors, tissues, thermometers, antihistamines, papers, notes and stained tea cups.

When Vickey asked what I was doing, I said, "Honey, if I told you—you'd never believe me anyhow."

And she said, "Try me!"

"Well, I'm writing a book—"

"You're kidding!" And as usual, the gale of laughter that always accompanied the disbelief that an invisible housewife could possibly have anything to say that the rest of the world would care to hear.

Once she got control of her laughter, she said, "What are you writing about?"

"Well, it has to do with me and Gene, our kids—and Jesus!" Then I sucked in my breath and wondered why in the world I ever said such a thing! This adorable little worldling would never understand a statement like that! But she became very serious. "Char, that's why I am calling, as I've really been going through something and I can't find anyone to help me. Your name keeps coming up in my mind and I heard you were some kind of religious nut. Can I talk to you someplace where it's quiet?"

I said, "Vickey—I'm sick with a fever, but I'd be happy to talk with you in a couple of days, okay?" I went back to chilling, sniffling and creating, when the telephone rang again. "Char, this is Vickey and I am sorry to bother you but I have to get right with the Lord right away. Can't I please come over?"

About thirty minutes later a sobbing heap fell into my arms when I opened the door. She was almost incoherent as she gasped for breaths in between sobs, and somehow, I was able to make out that she hadn't even known which house I lived in, but did know the name of the street and turned in at the first porch light she saw!

After she calmed down, we prayed together, and a new life started for Vickey. To have stopped Vickey from coming to my house that night would have been like trying to stop a baby from being born! She remained strong in her faith for several years, and we became very close. Then—I sensed a shift, a change. You know when others are drifting away from the faith, when they don't seem to be on the same wavelength you are any more. So many years went by and Vickey and her family moved to Texas. But still, being part of the same family meant we were often in touch via weddings, funerals and so forth.

But then I heard that things were not going too well as Vickey's son and his wife opted to drop out of the family scene and were not heard of for what wound up being a decade; then, her husband of thirty-two years left her for her best friend! The world seemed to come crashing down on her drooping shoulders. But from the ashes, her spirit rose again. When there is no place to go, but up—one has to do something. And Vickey rallied! She made the discovery that human love was never intended to take care of the void within. The emptiness, the ache, that hollow hole inside of her was made for God, and could never be satisfied by a male, food, entertainment, or any material thing.

Now, it is impossible to spend a few minutes with Vickey and not come away feeling better. She has learned the peace of forgiveness and the value of unconditional love, and was given this poem that has brought so many to tears because of its simplicity and power. It may not pass muster as to the rhythm and literary correctness, but it was inspired in Vickey, by God, and rose up through her pain to help heal her heart.

When Tears Fall like Rain

I'll dry your eyes,
I'll hold you tight.
I'll be here with you
All through the night.

So give me your pain.
It's all for my gain.
I'll make you whole once again.

I'll see you through,
Just watch what I do,
All because I love you.

Look in my face
And we'll win this race.
Always remember
It's at my pace.

Always be strong
As you walk along
And always remember
That I'm never wrong.

> Vickey Moore

You need to know that this came through a girl who would never answer a correspondence because she hated writing so much! Yet, now, she has journals full of loving thoughts sent to her direct from God.

For several years, Vickey worked in a Christian bookstore. People flocked to the store, just to spend some time with her. Pastors, street people, Baylor students, intellectuals, housewives, all were deeply touched by her sincere approach to their hearts.

I think one of the greatest gems she gave out goes something like this: Vickey realized she would often say that something "felt like crap" and one day, as she thought about this, she said, "Lord, is that word too crude for me to use? Is it dishonoring to you?" From a place deep inside of her, she found this bubbling up:

C—circumstances

R—Rob you of

A—Acceptance and

P—Peace—and circumstances are just crap! Circumstances change, but Truth never changes. And that was good enough for her.

While cleaning her chandelier one day, she wiped the film from a prism and realized how much better it would reflect the light, now that it was clean. To herself, she said, "Wow. Just like our hearts—in order for us to be transparent, our hearts have to be free of the grime of bitterness, resentment, and unforgiveness." As she continued cleaning, the thought

The Joy of Six! 71

came to her that one prism by itself is beautiful, but many are magnificent! A person has his own unique beauty, but a gathering of many beautiful people reflects His glory even more so.

She also related to me the experience of trying to burn a huge pile of cut limbs, and it just wouldn't burn. After a year or so, they touched a match to it, and a veritable explosion happened! She was asking God "Why?" and He replied—"Sap." The sap had to drain out. She was driving at the time, and the thought came to her –SAP—Self Appointed Purpose! There is no way we can "catch on fire" when we are full of self appointed purpose!

The girl can see a sign, pick up a shell, feel a texture—and she connects it with the Lord! What a way to live! Bravo, My Vickey—she has found the Victorious Secret!

Well, Vickey proved that particular book store to be a veritable chapel, and I found two different stores to be a chapel of sorts for me, as well.

Some years ago, I found myself in a hardware store, growing older in a very long line of customers. A small boy was ahead of me, clutching a bulging wrinkled bag in one hand and his purchase in the other.

Finally it was his turn to check out. I couldn't believe my eyes! Tenderly, he'd put his purchase on the counter and carefully extracted a piggy bank from the rumpled bag! Industriously, he began the process that we realized would go on for quite some time. Shake, shake...rattle, tinkle, clunk, shake. The checker looked dismayed, stammered and said, "Uh, this line's awfully long...better wait on that."

The little fellow's face fell. "But I have to get back! I left my little brother with the baby while she was sleeping so I could get here before you closed. I gotta get right back, but it's my mom's birthday, and we don't have no dad and I've saved a long time so I could get her this silverware. She's wanted it for so-o long."

People behind me started muttering, clearing throats and sighing. I felt he needed some encouragement.

"Hey Tiger...we'll wait. Don't get upset." I ignored the scowl I got from the check-out girl and turned to the four behind me, all stony personified impatience. Boldly, I blurted, "What if that was your son buying a gift for you? Would you be willing to wait?"

Sheepish grins. Downcast eyes. A spirit of camaraderie came over us and as I was speaking, I heard a low moan... the little guy was a dollar and fifty-six cents short!

"But I knowed I had enough," he stammered, as little grubby pockets were being ransacked and wrong-sided. For his attempt, three more cents, a rusty key and a bubble gum wrapper were added to the pile of coins on the counter.

I turned, hoping I wouldn't be facing a lynch mob as I scrabbled around in my purse for some change. A big black man behind me caught my eye as he handed me a quarter. Silently, the others in the line reached into their pockets. I grinned and made up the balance, slapped the handful of coins triumphantly on the counter top and said, "Here! Paid in full! Now hurry home to that baby."

When I was paying for my purchase, I turned to the faces behind me. Their expressions had been altered from indifference to a gentle softness. Strange, isn't it? Not one bit of Scripture had been quoted. Not one line of a sermon preached. But God met us there, that day in a hardware store, for you see, God is love and we felt Him there among us. I know those others felt Him, too.

Another time, many years ago, I was feeling smug and rather clever as I'd managed to make it through the door without my penny-conscious husband and my calculator-

The Joy of Six!

crazed son, both of whom nearly drove me to distraction by figuring out prices per ounce, which toilet tissue had the most footage, which jars have fake bottoms, which company is falsely advertising, what's on sale and what's for free! All I was after was a fairly well-balanced larder with just enough junk food thrown in to make life interesting.

As I was pushing my cart around, a very small boy, I'd say about eight or so, passed me. We smiled. We passed again, next aisle. I noticed he had a newspaper clipping circled. Grocery specials, no doubt. We smiled again, and I said, "Do you need any help?"

"Yeah, this special on paper toweling. I can't reach it... would you, please?" I placed the bargain in his basket thanking him as I wasn't aware of the bargain myself.

He went back to studying the list and newspaper clipping intently.

My anointed nosiness began to run. "Is your mother here in the store somewhere? You seem awfully young to be doing the shopping."

"No, I'm doing it by myself," he proudly announced. "My Dad'll pick me up." He squinted at his list again. "Say, can you read my mother's writing? See, she's gonna have another baby any minute now. Guess the doctor said she shoulda had it last week, and see, she cries a lot. She can hardly walk. We know she won't cry any more after the baby comes, 'cuz this is her fifth, and she always does this just before a baby comes. 'Specially if it don't come when the doctor says it's s'posed to."

Uh...been there, done that raced my thoughts.

"Well see, I'm the oldest," and it seemed as though he drew himself up an inch or so as he said it. "And I told my folks I could do this and...what did you say this word was?"

"Cleanser." By now, I'd turned my cart around and we found ourselves heading in the same direction.

I asked him if he minded and he said, "No, that would be fine." Together, we looked for the cleanser and he said, "We have to have a certain ounce size...the one on sale, here in the paper." We shifted all the cans of cleanser around until we found the right size. He put it into his cart like a trophy. He was being such a blessing to me!

We were both draped awkwardly over the frozen foods bin when I heard a strong cheerful voice behind us saying, "Hey, Sport!" (I hoped he wasn't addressing me). "How's it going?"

The little guy beamed proudly. "Got everything on mom's list, Dad. This here lady only had to help me once or twice...and when I couldn't read Mom's writing, she could."

The father gave his son a comradely hug, rumpled his hair, and turned to me and said, "Thanks for your help. I didn't know how he'd do. He didn't want me to leave his Mom. She really is miserable...did he tell you?"

I nodded.

"I'm sure it can't be long now...thanks, again," he said. And the two of them walked out of my life. But not out of my heart. Suddenly, the supermarket wasn't so super any more, without my little friend.

Oh, Laurie, Please Forgive Me!

I suppose it is better to write about an incident while the pain is still throbbing. Laurie, this pretty, unbelievably-young-looking grandmother/daughter of mine was perched atop a stool at my counter eating lunch with me. She is a much sought after professional painter and paperhanger. We had some time together recently, as she was helping me freshen up the interior of my home with some new paint and paper and touching up mistakes I'd made when I was trying to do it on my own before she got there. And that wasn't easy as she tried to do the touching up without my knowing she was doing it.

Yet, why would she try to keep me from knowing she was doing that? She learned early in life that I had eyes in the back of my head, not to mention helpers in every neighborhood to keep this many kids in tow. (We live just barely inside of our current addition. With six kids and a drum set, they wouldn't let us very far in).

Laurie is in a beautiful relationship right now, but it was not always so for her. Vickey happened to be visiting from Texas, and Laurie started sharing with her, almost as though she'd forgotten I was there.

She said, "I'd gone for counseling some time back, and the counselor thought it would be a good idea to put me under hypnosis to see if she could ferret out the reason that drove me to always pick men who treated me poorly emotionally."

"And...?" I said, trying to not register my surprise at this.

Laurie proceeded. "Mom, I hope this doesn't make you feel bad."

"Go on," I said as I prepared for a spat of afore-mentioned deep breathing and white-knuckling.

"Well, when she put me under, she took me through various times of my life. When we reached the point where I was about eight or so, I started squirming, feeling suffocated. When she asked me what was wrong, I said, "I don't know, but I keep hearing a motor go on...then it shuts off, and I feel gaspy."

"The counselor told me to take a couple of breaths, and we would move to another time. After the session, Lois, (the counselor) told me to go home and rest and to cover up good, as I would feel chilled.

"She was right. I went home, went to bed and was about to fall asleep when I heard that motor again. I put my hands over my ears, but it wouldn't stop...and then I sat bolt upright in bed, then ran to the phone to call Lois.

"Lois! I think I have it! That motor was the motor in our pool! I remembered a time when a cousin 'playfully' tried to drown me! He would hold me under until I thought sure I was going to drown, and then he'd pull me up again so I could catch a breath, and then he'd do it all over again. These cousins were older, and my mom thought someone was at the pool watching. When his mother finally saw what was going on, she started yelling at him, and he finally let me go, knowing that he was in big trouble. But I went into the house where mom was getting food ready, and I can still remember what she was wearing.

"I grabbed her, sobbing, and tried to tell her what he had

The Joy of Six!

done, but she just patted me on the head and told me not to take it so seriously...that when boys tease you like that, it's just their way of showing how much they love you. I think I took that to mean that a man didn't love me unless he wasn't nice to me! Could this be?"

I felt a bit faint. To think that something you said to a child at that age could bring about such chaos within her...it was soul-wrenching! I must have looked stricken, as Laurie said, "Mom, don't feel badly. Lois felt it was something else going on, too." But I felt so far away. I was remembering a time when a pastor had told me, "Charlene, you know we only tease the people we love." But to think I never took her sobbing seriously enough to realize he truly had almost drowned her! She certainly needed more than a pat on the head!

Oh, if I could only go back—if only I could have been the mother then that I am now...if only...but "if onlies" tend to rob you of the present moment, so I could only say, "Laurie, I am so sorry—I didn't know. I had no idea that a casual comment could go so deeply into the heart and lodge there for so many years, causing so much pain for you. I...am...so...sorry."

I have wept over this. And I think I have forgiven myself. It can't be undone. It is now a memory, a part of the dream that is past.

The very next day, Laurie came in and caught me in tears, as I happened to be watching a moving session on Oprah. It was a segment dealing with children relating the loving things their mothers did when they were dying of some terminal disease—how they laid plans to make the parting easier, and how grateful the children were for the mothers' great care and concern.

She watched the segment with me, and neither of us had

dry eyes as we sensed the tenderness being expressed. I was still very mellow from our exchange of the day before. I touched her lightly on the arm as she sat beside me on the sofa and whispered, "Laurie, can you forgive me for not being in a place where I could have been more supportive of you, all those many years ago? So often I have wished I could have had the spiritual maturity that I have now, when I was raising the lot of you. But I didn't...and you have all suffered, in some way or other. I have often wondered why God worked it out that you have physical strength for the task of child-rearing when you are young, even though there were times I was not too sure about that! But the wisdom thing came along waaay after the fact. It's one of the things I intend to mention to Him, when we chat face to face...but for the time being, I need to know that you have forgiven me."

A slow, tender little grin spread over her beautiful face as she reached over to hug me. "Oh, Mom—You silly thing! I forgave you ages ago for being less than perfect! That pretty well covered everything, now didn't it?"

We both had a tearful giggle over that, and all felt well in my world again. Once more, I made the discovery that "love covers a multitude of sins" and –picks up an awful lot of junk, I might add.

Celeb Escapades!

Once, I heard Dr. Robert Schuller give some grand advice. Well, actually I've heard him give grand advice on every broadcast, but this time, he was speaking directly to me for he said, "Don't be shy about introducing yourself to celebrities! They are people just like you and they love sharing their lives with others."

Well, I took that to heart, and since my sis and I were headed out to California in just a few weeks anyhow, I thought, "Why not contact Jessamyn West! She lives in Napa Valley, and we will be swinging right by her door! Of course! What a grand idea!" (At the time, I was devouring everything she'd ever written).

About a month before our arrival, I wrote Ms. West a note, asking her if I could stop by to meet her. In the note, I mentioned that I was a Hoosier as I know she was partial to Hoosiers, even though she had lived so many years in California. Her early years were spent around Seymour, Indiana. I told her that, "although we have never met you will recognize me as a Hoosier as I will be clutching a can of mace, with a rape whistle hanging around my neck!"

She wrote a friendly note back, saying that Yes, she didn't normally do this, but that she would agree to meet me.

On the day I'd scheduled a visit with Ms. West, my sister was in the throes of a terrible cold. She said, "That dear lady is quite old, and I don't want to expose her to this, so do you mind going alone?"

I didn't, so I did—go visit her alone, I mean. It seemed so simple—I had only to stay on one road to get there, but the road went on forever, with twists and turns and gaps and canyons, fence posts and prairies, vineyards, valleys, creeks and vastnesses beyond anything this little Hoosier hayseed had ever seen, and as the sky deepened I knew I'd never see my sister again!

But I finally got to Ms. West's house, timidly knocked at the door and was met by a smiling, housewifely semblance of soft wrinkles and laughter that collapsed into vibrancy as she greeted me and invited me in. We shook hands and she waved me toward a seat as she said, "Well, my dear, this is most unusual, as I don't normally invite strangers into my home. Now, how did this come about? Do we know one another?"

I laughed, and told her that no, we didn't know one another, but that my coming to see her was Dr. Bob Schuller's idea. I then explained his little bit of logic with her and mentioned that I had sent her a note asking if I could come by.

She looked thoughtful, then said, "Tell me again, you wrote this note when?"

"Oh, about a month ago," I chirped.

At that point, she threw her hands in the air, and said, "Oh, well then—that explains it. If you wrote a month ago, then I've already forgotten it!"

It was an unforgettable forty-five minutes. Well, at least for me, it was. We talked about writing and her philosophy on life—it was so enlightening. But the thing I remember most was her telling of being a bit ticked with the media.

"Charlene, they just won't listen to me! They keep putting my age at 81, and my dear girl, I am not 81—I am 83! And I am so very tired! My husband is 85, and he loves traveling in our motor home. I can't seem to make him understand how that tires me."

They laid her to rest the next year, as I recall. But what a legacy she left behind!

Her books have always been a great inspiration to me and I cherish this memory.

My only other brush with a celebrity happened back in 1989. Unless you want to count the time I smiled at Wayne Dyer when we passed in a hallway, but I hardly think he remembers that! Well, I'd taken a trip with that sister of mine, again, and I read the entire Carol Burnett book to her and our friend Mary, who drove so I could read.

In that book, I found a picture of Carol Burnett's great-grandmother's home in San Antonio, Texas. I kept glancing at it, and I told Lauraine that it would make a really cute quilted wall-hanging—something that I was doing at the time while waiting for the writing juices to rev up.

She said, "Hey, why don't you do that, then send it to her?"

It turns out that she was "right on" as she has been so many times in my life. I did do the wall-hanging, and saw that it had some merit, a kind of cute sparkle that Carol Burnett might enjoy, so I did what any seasoned writer would do. I wrote to Carol, asking her if she'd like to have the wall-hanging as a gift. Being a published author, I had the good sense to write in care of the publishing company, as that is how I got my so-called fan mail.

Of course I wrote the letter that would hold Carol mesmerized for at least twenty minutes, of which said letter, I am sure she never saw...but I did get a call from her publicist. It was late on a Saturday night, about eleven o'clock Indiana time. I was alone as Gene was out of town.

When the phone rang, I picked it up, sleepily, as I was zonked. When I said "Hullo," and not too enthusiastically, I might add. I heard what sounded vaguely like heavy breathing, as the person on the other end kept attempting to get my name right. "Uhhh...eh, phew—Patter—Uh, Pot—Patterdom?" Well, I figured that was close enough considering the hour.

"Yes," I responded, sleepily.

"Alright. Good. Now—uh, recently you sent a photo of a quilted wall-hanging to Ms. Burnett—is this correct?"

Then I was into heavy breathing! "Yessss,"—I gushed, as I fell back into my pillows.

"Okay. Now, in this letter—"

As he was gathering his thoughts, I churned out some of my own, thinking—Those kids! They are pulling one over on me! They have set me up! I'm gonna strangle 'em first chance I get! So I was about to get cheeky with him, until I heard him mention something that no one knew was in the letter, but me!

When I realized this was a genuine star-studded call, I felt perspiration breaking out all over me as I quaked and shook! And giggled and made a general buffoon of myself.

Well, within just a few days, I shipped my masterpiece to Carol Bunrett, via this publicist's address (in the event I might have tucked in a bomb, too, I suppose). Actually, I had no dealings with her, except for a nice handwritten thank-you note complete with the tiny "e" she always tacks on the tail of her signature, to keep peace in the family between her mother and grandmother, as they continually argued as to whether or not her name was Carol or Carole. I might also add that Carol Burnett sent a most generous check to our church building fund! That was pretty exciting for all of us, but the heart-warming part was hearing the publicist extol the virtues of Ms. Burnett.

He said, "You know, I have worked as a publicist for many of these people here in Hollywood, and some of them are very difficult to work for. But I can honestly tell you that Carol is one of the nicest, kindest people I have ever met, and it is a great pleasure to work for someone like her. She is very sentimental about her childhood and anything from her past means so much to her. She lived in this home with her great-grandparents until she was eight or so...she will get all teary-eyed when this arrives."

During a later conversation, I heard that her interior decorator had taken the wall-hanging and put it in a wonderful antique frame, under glass. No, I never had any dealing with Carol Burnett, but whenever I see her on TV, I feel like someone who is hugging a great secret, and think Oh, wow. Today, she may have walked past the wall-hanging I did for her!

That is pretty much a wrap up of my celebrity escapades, but there is one more incident I'd love to share. I am indebted to someone who goes to church with me for this one. Barb is an elegant lady whom we all admire. Her accent reminds one of soft breezes and romance, as she was born and raised in Trinidad, in the West Indies. Sadly, both her parents and a much beloved aunt died when she was ten, and she was lovingly taken in by her grandmother. Her grandmother knew she was still very grief-stricken, so she took her to the first movie Barb had ever seen. She said, "I will never forget the experience! I was totally mesmerized by the whole panorama before me! But most of all, I was taken by this gorgeous man with salt and pepper hair, and he became the man of my dreams. It was Jeff Chandler, right there before me bigger than life! When cousins and playmates chided me for being taken with this obviously older man, they would say, "You are such a silly thing! You should be dreaming about Farley Granger, not someone who is already turning gray!" I remember giving a little flip to my hair, like sassy little girls do and muttering 'I don't care what you think! It makes no difference, because—someday, Jeff Chandler is coming to have tea with me!' Of course, they laughed me to scorn, but I never gave up on the idea that this wonderful man would come have tea with me. As a child, it was something I thought about often.

"Then, while I was living in the Philippines at the age of twenty-one, I believe, a former yard boy who had worked for us became a chauffeur driver. He happened to be driving Jeff Chandler around one day, and he proceeded to tell him about the little girl who told everyone that Jeff Chandler was coming to have tea with her someday. Playfully, he said,' She now lives here—you really should meet her! Would you like to do that while you are here?

Jeff Chandler thought that would be a lark, so a meeting was set. Barb said, "I remember the meeting was arranged for two o'clock in the afternoon and when he came into my home, it was as though we had known one another for years! We had such a lively chat! It is such a fond memory for me. And doesn't it prove how the power of the mind can bring about a deep inner knowing, if you truly believe? As a little girl, I never wavered in my belief that he would come visit me, someday."

When I shared this story with my daughter Laurie, she said, "Mom, do you remember when I went on that trip to Haiti with the church? When we were sitting in the international section, waiting to board our plane, the girls spotted a handsome young man with long flowing, beautiful hair, and they got all excited, as they were certain he was

The Joy of Six!

someone famous. They were all too chicken to approach him so guess who they sent? Well, I went to him and asked him what his name was. He smiled, and said, 'Roger Daltry'—but I thought he said "Roger Doctry' because he had a thick accent, so I said, 'Oh, Roger Doctry' and he grinned, and said, 'Yes, that's right.' He must have realized that I didn't have a clue as to who he was, so we chatted for quite awhile, and mostly he wanted to know what all the young people were going to do while in Haiti. I told him about the orphanage we were going to help paint, and how we'd be making curtains and helping with little ones... he was so interested, but he never mentioned his music or what he did. This tall, really pretty redhead came up to us, and her arms were loaded with shopping bags, boxes—and she was loaded with jewelry. He introduced me to her—his wife, and she started chatting with us, too.

"When it came time to board, he patted me and said,' Laurie, I will never forget you,' so I went back to my group, and they were all excited—they asked, 'Laurie, who was that?' I said, 'Oh, Roger Doctry—no one I ever heard of...'They all squealed and giggled like seventeen year old girls do, and said, 'Laurie! That was Roger Daltry, of the WHO! Didn't you know that?' and then I got kind of weak in the knees, because we'd had such a fun chat together—and I wondered why people were stepping up and taking pictures of us! I thought they were taking pictures of the people behind us! But you know what, Mom? I think he enjoyed our visit, simply because I wasn't looking at him as a celebrity, but as just another normal person, needing some distraction from the tedium of travel. I remember the sly grin when he said, 'Yes, Roger Doctry—that's the name.'"

Oh, Brother!

I married an "only child." Often, when asked by others if he might not have liked having a sibling, I have heard him say, "Well, it is difficult to miss something you never had."

I truly miss something I once had—my three brothers. They all died while in their sixties, so I was elated to see my sister make it into her seventies, and I am also pleased to know I approach my seventieth year in very good health, as well. It is also difficult remembering that I am now older than they ever got to be, for I was –am still—the baby of the family.

When my brother Roger Kendall was very ill with leukemia, someone gave me twenty dollars to send to him in Florida. (This community had lovingly started a fund for him). I called Rog to tell him, but weakly he said, "No, Char. My needs are being met and we are doing fine. Keep the money in Elkhart and find someone who needs some help there."

This didn't surprise me, as Rog had such a soft spot in his heart for this community. He was a retired policeman who had delivered babies in squad cars, took crippled children to Chicago ball games, played Santa at Christmas, helped drunks sober up, took delinquents into his home, became a clown in his spare time, helped out at the Bashor Boy's home—and his crowning glory was the huge parking tickets he made out for children in the hospital if their stay

The Joy of Six!

was very long. The tickets had a place to check if you didn't take your medicine cheerfully, didn't smile, didn't sleep well, or grumped around. This became such an important function, he was granted an extended lunch hour from the police department, so he could make the hospital rounds daily.

I forgot about the money and Rog's request for a few days, but when I remembered it, I also thought of someone who worked at the welfare department. I called Shirley and told her about the money. She said, "That sounds like Rog, doesn't it? Actually, I have a black family in mind. The mother abandoned the children and they are being raised by their grandmother and a disabled father. School is about to start, and they need shoes."

I gave the money to Shirley and a few days later she called me. "Char, this has been a great experience! You won't believe what happened. I called the grandmother and told her to get the kids ready as we were going for some shoes. Char, she cried...but before I'd called her, I did the strangest thing. I called our big department store and asked for the manager. When he heard what Roger had done, he said 'I will leave word that we will match the money."

"Later that afternoon, I had three black teenagers in tow. A cheerful salesman helped us plough through mounds of shoes and lots of explaining to the teenagers as to why we should stay with the more practical shoes. When we totaled the bill, we were still fourteen dollars short, even with the generous offer from the store. At exactly the same time, the salesman and I reached into our billfolds and split the difference! God multiplied that $20 into fifty- four dollars! (This was back in the seventies, so that would be equal to much more than that today).

Roger was so pleased. At the time, I had a wonderful

black woman by the name of Mary who came in to help me clean. When she made the discovery that I was "Roger Kendall's baby sister" she got all teary-eyed and chuckled deeply. She dreamily waxed my dining room table as she related tale after tale of the times he had come to rescue her. I knew from obvious knife scars on her arms that she had been in a barroom brawl a time or two, but she seemed to be such a gentle soul now. I watched her eyes tear up as she said, "Oh, how I'd love the chance to try and knock that dear brother down, just one more time...he was sooo good to me!"

During the depression, sources of food were pretty scarce here. Roger wanted to go join the CCC's (Civil Conservation Corps) but had no money for the trip to California. Being resourceful, he bought a five-gallon gas can. He carefully cut a neat ample door in the side and attached two small hinges. He stuffed it full of a few clothes and necessities and off he went, thumbing his way across the country with his gas can by his side! His picture got into many newspapers across the country, replete with wide grin and handy can alongside.

And so, I became known as "Roger Kendall's baby sister." He'd even managed to make me somewhat famous before I got into high school, for in almost every class I attended on that awesome day-of-all-days as a very green sophomore, I'd see teachers write down my name, and they'd say, "oh, so you're the one...I remember the day Roger brought you to school in a baby carriage." Not exactly what you wanted to hear when hoping to look svelte, mature, and sophisticated! But it seems that Roger had a penchant for skipping school. Every time he was called on the carpet before the principal, he'd look somewhat pitiful and murmur that his "mother was sick" and he had to tend to "the little baby sister."

Then one day, Mom really did get sick. He didn't want the folks to know what was going on, so he bundled me up and told Mom he wanted to take me to school and show me off. It created quite a stir when they saw him coming down the halls of old Elkhart High with one of those old-fashioned baby carriages, the straw-looking kind that belonged to a former Victorian era.

He pushed me around to several classes until the principal heard of his shenanigans; when questioned, Roger just shrugged his shoulders and looked innocent. "Like I told you, my mom has been sick and I..." The principal laughed and slapped him on the back and told him to take me back home and to BE SURE to come in the next day...alone!

Ah, my bother Bobby. The one thing I do remember about him while growing up, was the difficult time he had waking up. To help keep my mother from losing her sanity, he devised the alarm to win all awards. It was an elaborate system that involved tons of marbles whirling through a chute to hit a tin dishpan that was made to wobble so the marbles would keep clacking and clunking together before they were let through another chute; then belched out the marbles in a tin container close to his head, which of course, woke everyone in the house—but Bob. Bob always reminded me of Danny Kaye. He loved to make people laugh. He lived out of state for most of my growing up years, but when his wife died, he wound up on our doorstep every other weekend, he was so lonely.

After several months of widower status, he met a lovely woman named Elaine. They lived in the same neighborhood, so they weren't exactly strangers. Just a week or so prior to their wedding, Bob wound up in the hospital with what the doctor's diagnosed as a "mushy heart." As he had to remain in the hospital, and the staff loved him so much the doctor said, "Bob, why don't you and Elaine get married here in the hospital? We'd love to be part of it." So that is what they did. The nurses tied juice cans to his wheel-chair, made toilet paper bows and blew up rubber gloves for a festive touch on the dessert table.

Bob had looked extremely pale during the ceremony. I asked Gene if we couldn't spend the night in his area so I could visit him one more time in the hospital before we returned home. When we arrived at the hospital and stepped into his room, he was sleeping soundly and his color looked more normal. We weren't going to bother him, but a nurse insisted on it. "Oh, do wake him! He will want to see you. He can go back to sleep after you leave—Bob, you have company!" And before I knew it, she left the room and he was reaching out for a big hug and grinning at me from ear to ear.

He said, "Here, Char—come sit on the edge of my bed— I am so glad you stayed over!" And we chatted about his plans for his return home, and some trips we intended to take as a foursome the next month, and he kept patting my hands as I sat there. He had me read from the little booklet that explained how to live one's life with "a mushy heart" and what would be involved. He'd been told that more bed rest, some mild exercise and fresh air would be the ticket and soon have him totally recovered.

The nurse came swinging back into his room with some clean linen. She stopped dead in her tracks, saw me on the edge of his bed, and said, "Well! I declare!"

Sheepishly, I hopped off the bed apologizing, "Uh-oh! Hospital rules, right? Oh, I am so sorry!"

But she laughed and said, "No, not that at all. It's just that he had informed us all that that was his 'wedding bed' and no one was to touch it! You must really have some

The Joy of Six!

clout with him!"

I hated to leave, but had to, as my son Jamie was getting married the next weekend, and there was so much yet to be done. I talked to Bob on Tuesday and told him I'd call after the wedding and tell him all about it. On Thursday, as I was getting ready to have a shower that night for the new bride I got a call from Elaine, Bob's wife.

"Charlene, you'd better sit down. Bobby just died." I slid to the floor and don't remember much after that, but I managed to pull myself together in order to get through the shower. Bob was cremated, so there were no immediate services. I miss him so much.

Allen was the third born. He was a royal tease while my sister and I were growing up, but his charm made it possible for us to finally forgive him. Allen had an incredible knack putting couples together to the point that he was developing quite a reputation—his successes were so varied and thriving.

Once, when he'd stopped by my house for coffee, he was proudly telling of his latest accomplishment in the cupid department. Gene seemed thoughtful for a moment then he said, "You know, my barber was mentioning that he'd sure like to settle down and find some nice girl to share his life with. Allen, you got any ideas?"

Allen grinned and said, "Yeah, as a matter of fact, we have the nicest girl working in the office...I was teasing her the other day, telling her I was going to be on the lookout for some nice guy for her! What a great coincidence!" We began to plot our plans, and I felt excited to be a part of one of his strategic moves.

A couple of days later he called, and cheerily said, "Char, I talked to the gal in our office, and she was a bit hesitant, but I think she is interested! But you know I didn't catch your barber's name, only that is was 'Joe.' So, Joe who?"

"Oh, it's Joe—Bazzoco, I think. Yes, that's it."

There seemed to be a long silence. Then, I heard a deep roar that started first in his stomach, and made its way to my ear. "What's so funny?" I squeaked.

He was laughing so hard, he could hardly speak. "Her name—her name is Mary—Bazzoco! When I'd told her this guy's name was Joe, but that I didn't know his last name, she said, 'Oh, I have a brother Joe! Hope this guy is as nice as he is!' Can you believe this?" And he went into another spasm of mirth.

Well, needless to say, I didn't meddle with anyone else's heartstrings after that. And Joe, all by himself, found a lovely gal and they are still married, even though this happened so many years ago. That, in itself is a miracle in this day and age.

Well, your life won't be complete until you meet my sister, Lauraine. If you were to step into her living room she would be so proper and quaint but let me tell you— she has to be one of the funniest human beings that God ever created. We are six years apart in age, and she doesn't remember much about me when we were growing up, because I'd become very good at becoming invisible. I tell people we didn't speak until we got married, but that's only because she had to work hard all of her life because my mother was so near death many times.

Because of this, Lauraine had to give up her dream of being a nurse. When her position in a local factory office was dissolved, she finally had the chance to follow her dream down the bedpan trail of life.

Part of her training required working with geriatrics. She liked this idea, in case she did something really stupid as she felt confident they'd forget it ever happened. As she

The Joy of Six! 93

struggled while giving a bath for the first time, straddling herself over the side-bar, a tiny little voice said, "Dearie, wouldn't it be easier if you let that bar down?" To which Lauraine smiled, and mumbled, "Eh, yes—yes, that would be easier—thank you," as she sheepishly lowered it. After the bath, she fumbled about again, squeezing that blood pressure cup for all she was worth—over and over again. The tiny little voice cleared her throat again, and whispered, "Dearie—wouldn't it be easier if you put those things in your ears? That's how the others--" But by then, Lauraine was laughing uncontrollably as she hugged the dear old soul and started all over again. This time, she got it right!

Another time, she was doing the required mouth exam on the ward. As she spoke to one man, she saw this terribly red, sore-looking spot in his mouth, so she asked him to 'open wide' for a better view. He clamped his mouth shut as tight as he could and refused to open it for her. Alarmed by what she had seen, she ran for the supervisor, and the two of them were about to investigate when he angrily held up his hand. He sputtered, "You leave me alone! This here is my cherry from my roll at breakfast, and yer not gittin' it!"

Another time, as they were learning the hygiene routine for mouth care, Lauraine had to clean the teeth of a gentleman who was comatose. Carefully, she extracted the upper set of teeth and cleansed them then she reached in to gently release the bottom set of teeth. For some reason, they were sealed in tighter than the others. She kept trying, and in exasperation, she went, again, for her supervisor, who agreed that yes, these teeth had to be cleaned as well. The supervisor found the teeth to be as stubborn so she put one knee up on the bed and pulled with all her might. Then she squealed, "Oh my god! These are HIS OWN TEETH! Who would have believed it! They look too perfect! (Word of advice—should you have to put anyone in the hospital, be sure to specify whether or not they have a FULL set of false teeth, and put it in writing!).

But the most hilarious incident involved the bath care of an old gent. It was time for his shower, so two student nurses put him in one of the special chairs they have for showering that was designed with a hole in the seat. It was Lauraine's assignment so she wheeled him out into the hallway as she made her way to the showers, only to hear someone behind her exclaiming, "Oh, wait, Mrs. Holycross—please wait just a minute!" A senior nurse came running up with a sheet, and was about to swoop it around the old gent, as she told Lauraine, "It really is QUITE necessary to drape them, and if you'll step back, you'll see what I mean—just remember, next time."

Embarrassed, Lauraine went on with her assigned duty. She scrubbed him above the waist, and then politely asked him if he could do 'his other parts' but he turned a pitiful, helpless face her way, indicating that he could do nothing for himself. So, she proceeded to avert her eyes, humming a little aimless tune, while sudsing around in the 'nether regions." Half-soaked herslf, she made him comfortable, draped him again, and wheeled him back to his room. As soon as they arrived in his room and got close to his lounger, he hopped out of the wheel chair, picked up his newspaper, flicked on his light—and winked at her! But in spite of all this, she has a great bedside manner and can scrub a back better than anyone I know.

Didn't I tell you that the people in my life were interesting?

One time, during a women's retreat, I'd suggested that for "ice-breakers" we might all go around and remember some humorous moments we'd had in our lives. I was struck by

The Joy of Six! 95

the sad statement one woman made. She said, "You know, I can't remember any funny things ever happening in my life." I had trouble fathoming such a thing, because humor is all around us, waiting for us to gasp and splutter our way into the next moment! It peeks at us from the mirror, from our children, from our friends—it binds and weaves its way into our conversations, into our dreams—it is everywhere to be enjoyed! It can happen even before you realize it.

My son Mark was feeling a bit nervous about meeting his girlfriend's parents for the first time. When they asked him if he wanted something to drink, he smiled, then stammered, "Oh, I'm fine thank you—but I'd take a glice of ass-water, if you don't mind!" That was indeed a "glice-breaker." But you should have heard what Mindy's mom did with "Pharaoh's heart" in front of her Sunday school class!

Picture This!

Picture this: My zany 75 year old sister Lauraine and her respectable husband Mer, stranded by the roadside in Michigan with a sharp-looking but broken down Buick that balked from the strain of pulling their dune buggy, of all things!

My sister, wanting to be helpful stood by the road, going through gyrations that looked like she was twisting her ear off while yodeling through her fist. Her children informed her that she would have been better understood, had she stuck her thumb in her ear, and her pinky up her nose, letting jet-setters whizzing by know that she needed phone assistance. Probably someone from her own generation got her message, for soon a young, very caring policeman came by and, seeing their dilemma, soon had a tow truck on the scene.

My sister said, "People lined up on the highway—they thought it was a parade! The tow-truck was pulling the Buick, which was pulling the dune buggy, and the officer was escorting all of this in his police car behind. He wouldn't let us sit in the dune buggy, as he didn't want people to think we might be the clowns in this parade, so Mer got into the front seat of the police car and I was helped into the back seat by the nice-looking young officer.

"It didn't take us long to get to where the car needed to be towed, but once we got there, Mer and the officer leapt

The Joy of Six!

out of the car to speak with the man towing our string of cars. I realized Mer needed to get some information and instructions, so I quietly waited in that interesting car, looking at all the gadgets on the console, watching lights blink and listening to radios squawking, and to pass the time, I thought about all the different things the instrument panels might be for. This was fine, for awhile—but I soon became aware of a growing need to answer a call of nature, and having drawn very close to this bladder after all these years, I knew it could be very demanding in very short order. I needed to get out of that car, very quickly—however, I made the discovery that the back doors of police cars don't even open from the inside!

"Of course I called for Mer, but he couldn't have heard me if we'd been standing in a telephone booth together because he doesn't hear too well, and now, added to his loss of hearing was the drone of the tow truck, plus several other huge vehicles now adding their poisons to the atmosphere as well as the sound level. All the men on the scene were rapt in the wonder of the dune buggy and other bits of very loud machinery cranking out their own symphonies to better fascinate these male creatures.

"Naturally, fear gave birth to claustrophobia as I beat on windows and strained my vocal chords while visions of awful things happening whirled through my head. I could hear a voice down at "Central" and I pleaded with her to help me, but of course all she could say, was "Car #52— Where are you?" as I hadn't the foggiest as to what button I needed to push, nor could I reach it if I had known!

"Panic set in, so I knew I had to make a dive for it! I muttered, 'Console, prepare thyself—I'm going overboard!" I swung one leg over; got tangled in wires, phone jacks, and headsets; saw Tic-Tacs rolling to the floor boards; straddled the back of the seat, while I caught my breath; then gave an earth-shattering shudder as I hove the rest of me to landward ho! I couldn't believe that I'd been goofy enough to wear a skirt on this, of all days!

"As I tumbled clumsily into the front seat, managing to wedge myself under the steering wheel, while losing a shoe and all my dignity, I thought I saw a tiny camera winking at me! Inwardly, I groaned and thought, 'Oh, no—I am going to be featured on America's Funniest Videos, and I won't even live to see it if I die here of embarrassment!' as I reached for the door and dumped myself unceremoniously out on the ground. After a bit of deep breathing, I was able to get myself upright, brush myself off, retrieve my shoe, and the men still didn't notice me!

"I walked a bit unsteadily toward them, trying to regain my composure. The formerly-thought-of as 'nice, young policeman' turned around, saw me and said, 'Oh—Oh, I forgot all about you!'

"With all the dignity I could muster, I said, 'Young man, I am well aware of that! Now, unless you carry Depends as a staple, I suggest you find me a bathroom, quickly!"

As I have observed this kind of thing happening to my dear sister for most of her life, I don't really feel like she is an accident going somewhere to happen, but more like a comedy going someplace to be shared! She has brought much joy to my life, and to the lives of many others. Her knack for seeing the humorous in everything has endeared her to all who know her. Lauraine, I owe you so much—thanks for being my sister. I know I can always Depend on you!

My Garage Door Opener

Every time I use my garage door opener, I am filled with awe. How can this be? How can I simply push a tiny button and this huge cavity opens before me? Then, I maneuver my car inside, and poof! I push the button and the door goes down! I can make it work from inside the house, or even around the corner! Majestic!

Frequencies, Gene tells me. And that fills me full of awe, too, as there must be so much out there that we don't even know about. Energy. Varying energies, it seems. Different wave-lengths. We even use that when expressing frustration, as in "you just don't seem to be on the same wave-length as I am!"

And then an acupuncturist tumbles into my life; she explains to me what the Chinese have been saying for over five thousand years, that we are surrounded by a subtle energy field, and thanks to, of all things, quantum physics, it now is a proven fact. Everything is energy! Even objects that appear to be not moving, such as rocks and some couch potatoes—all have swirling molecules, and at the center of the molecules, there are atoms with little electrons zinging away as they twirl around the atom! And they are all made from and contain—Light! (This little light of min-n-ne—I'm gonna let it shin-ne...This little ...well, you get it, I'm sure.)

Take our feelings, for instance. Our e-motions, no less.

Our energies in motion, that is. Isn't it comforting to know that we can take control of these surging, pulsing, running rampant feelings just by changing a thought? For instance, you just mopped and waxed the kitchen floor and your toddler spills the milk. (Now, this is when I became aware that God was doing something special in my life—when I started being nice to my children, even though there were no strangers around). Naturally, this sticky mess spills some despair into the heart of any tidy housekeeper. But, if you take a deep breath, clean the toddler up first and put them in a safe place, you can let go of that despairing feeling while allowing love to flood your soul as you pick the little one up. You have dissolved the weaker energy by flooding it with the strongest energy of all—Love. And if you will actually time yourself while you are cleaning up the spilt milk, you will find it was hardly worth the few moments of despair you indulged in. It is all a matter of choice!

It was a thrilling day for me when I discovered that not only was I responsible for my feelings, but that I could make choices very quickly to make things better. Like the other day—can't remember why, but I felt a feeling of dread creeping up on me. With authority I said (aloud!)"Alright, we are not even going there, okay? Whatever is before me can be greeted with enthusiasm and joy—no room for any dread to roost here today!" And that quickly, it was gone!

It hasn't always been easy for me. I remember a time when as a young mother, I felt so harried, so burdened with responsibilities. I developed a "poor me" attitude, and kept saying something to the effect that I "felt like I'd bumped into a brick wall and couldn't go on." There seemed to be no one around to tell me that if I would just change the words I was speaking and the thoughts I was thinking; that if I chose to see my life from a different perspective, those feelings would melt away and be replaced by something much more positive and comfortable.

I told the doctor that I felt badly because so many older women were saying, "But dear, these are the best years of your life!" The doctor quietly took my hand and said, "It's because they have forgotten."

Now I look back and realize that those could have been the best years of my life...if one of those dear women would have loved me enough to help me change the way I was thinking—and talking

I don't mean to fault those older women, but truly—I needed some guidance at this time. Well, God—being God like He is—sent me some guidance in the form of two pastors—one from Australia (my nephew David) and one from our local church. They sensed I was having a difficult time, so both, over a cup of coffee, tenderly began to inform me that I had everything I would ever need, right here inside of me; all the love, wisdom, peace—I was equipped with everything I would ever need from my conception. All I had to do was to recognize and remove the "blocks" that kept me from seeing and enjoying all of this, in order for me to have a "wonderful life." They described my "blocks" as being resentments, grievances, jealousies, comparisons, aversions, anger—anything that smacked of disharmony.

All of this time spent straightening out my spiritual kinks required a lot of energy, so the general consensus was that a night out on the town was in order. So after dinner, a car full of us went to see the movie "Oz." This included my nephew, his wife, gobs of children and half the neighborhood. During the most touching part of the movie, when most people were shedding tears because of the tender scene where Dorothy declares to Auntie Em that "everything I have ever needed or wanted is right here in my own backyard—all the love, the joy, the peace..." or at least that is how I remember it—Well, the whole carload began to snicker and giggle as my niece leaned over and whispered, hoarsely—"Well, now you've heard this message form two pastors, a scarecrow, a tin man, a lion and a girl clicking her heels together—did you finally get the message?"

Sometimes, I feel our moods are set by the words we use, for even words convey their own special energy. For instance, if I have a project going, (wallpapering, redoing a floor, or painting the house) I never refer to it as "work." The word "work" carries a trainload of stuff like drudgery, labor, heaviness, have-to-do-ness, sweating—but a Project? A Project is something that can be undertaken with enthusiasm, fun planning, excitement and real joy, because you have given it great thought, you have played with it in your mind, and you can love the feeling of accomplishment as it happens before your very eyes! A Project has a beginning, and middle and an end! What fun! But "work" feels like it might drag on forever.

And take the word "chaos." It's kind of what happens when grandchildren arrive in swarms, but I have found it sets much better with my insides if I stop referring to it as "chaos" which carries the weight of non-organization and scatteredness with it. By attaching the words "happy activity" to the scene, I just feel better.

Actually, our most natural state is pure Joy. (Observe babies for a short time, if you doubt my words.) We just don't experience the Joy that is available to all of us because we have been so conditioned by well-meaning parents, teachers and siblings to think a different way; we either learn or observe competition, striving, jealousy, people-pleasing, manipulation, gossiping and slandering, mixed with just enough kindness and goodness, so the messages

The Joy of Six!

are varied and hard to decode at times.

Oh, my. If Don ever gets wind of all this philosophizing I have done here, he will shake his head, sigh deeply and say, "too teachy-preachy, Mom. It will never fly." So as you can see, my heavenly Father has given me this bunch of great kids and relatives to always keep me humble. And if that doesn't do the trick, then God uses incidents.

I remember the time I was eating in a posh restaurant, just after a speaking engagement in some big city. The Board had taken me to lunch, so I had very daintily asked for a small chef salad, which was a bit deceptive of me because I was really hankering for a big ol' plate of lasagna.

Well, when the salad came, I saw that the only thing small about it was the round-bottomed wooden bowl they had put it in. As to what would happen when I put a blob of dressing on it remained to be seen. But not for long, for in about three seconds, the salad—remained to be seen—all down the front of me. When I tried to cut the huge chunks of lettuce with my knife, that round-bottomed bowl catapulted into the air—HIGH, into the air—and I found strings of cheddar draped in the hinges of my glasses, chunks of Roquefort entwined in my jewelry, and a recalcitrant tomato in the bend of my elbow. My sister was traveling with me at the time, and she enjoyed the faux pas immensely.

I also recall a time when I was on a flight from Cleveland to Miami. The flight attendants made the discovery that I was a published author and made a big fuss over me. They had me autograph copies of my book for them and the entire crew signed a "Friendly Skybird" hat for me. Believe me, it was quite a heady experience, so God served up a little humble pie-in-the-sky for me when I got home.

Now, realize—this incident happened back in the good old days when men still filled the gas tanks for helpless women like myself. I pulled up to the gas station in my son's car I had borrowed for the afternoon. The attendant said, "M'am, your tank is on the other side of your car."

"Oh, my"—I stammered. "Borrowed car, y' see—heh, heh" as I pulled ahead, made a big U-turn and pulled up on the other side of the gas pump ramp. He stepped between the pumps and said, "Lady, I don't know how to tell you this—but your tank is still on the other side of the car!" Well, I can't remember if I circled the block, or what I did do, but he finally got that tank filled. I presented him with my credit card. He glanced at the name, and exclaimed, "Say—nice to meet you! I just finished reading your book the other day!"

Pleased as all git-out, I fluffed my hair a bit, and said, "Oh, really? How wonderful! That really makes my day. How did you happen to run across my book?"

"Oh," he grunted, as he leaned across the windshield to do that other very old-fashioned service we used to get, as he said, "Well, see—my Dad is a trash collector, and the other day I helped him with the collections, and sure enough—there it was, on top of the heap.." and we chanted together "as big as life!"

I was laughing hysterically as I drove away, as he was muttering, "Oh, now don't feel bad, I mean, my mother read it and my aunt, and let's see—oh, yeah, my sis read it, too—it was a REAL good book, lady!" I drove away envisioning this smelly little mass of papers threaded throughout with dried spaghetti—oh, well—the Lord can recycle my books any old way he wants. At least it was still bearing fruit, even if it was peach pits and banana peelings.

Now, where was I? Oh, the garage door opener...how did we get clear over here? Hmm-mm. I think it's that "seventies" thing creeping up on me.

Remembering...I do lots of that, these days

Kisses, hugs, doors slamming, cars starting, gym bags bumping, last-minute checks for lunch tickets, field trip slips, baseball mitts, briefcases...one by one they stood before me, as before a tribunal—"Mom, does my hair look alright?"—"Do I look dumb in this?"—"Mom, does this make me look fat?"—"Be here when I get home, okay, Mom?"—as they left the trauma center we called "home" to seek the warmth and security of their particular peer groups that made the cold, impersonal world a habitable place for them to grow in.

And me? Quietly, after the noisy exodus, I would admit to myself that I had just made it with flying colors through one of the day's most trying hours as I slipped into my favorite mulling-over place, tucked my inexpensive robe around my too expansive body while sipping very expensive coffee from an un-exquisite mug. For a few treasured and blessed moments, I listened to the dust settle, pipes wheeze, fluorescents choke and splutter, while drinking in the stillness and loving it. (If you have never heard the dust settle at your house, it's only because you've never raised six children. If you had, you'd have heard it plummeting earthward like falling meteors).

The Mary part of me kicked in as I talked to the Minister of my Interior, thanking Him for these experiences and relishing a few quiet pages of something spiritual to give me some direction and stamina for the day—but before too long, the Martha part of me started to chide, and I knew if I sat there too long, I'd have to pry the hot chocolate cups up with a table knife.

I put down the books that meant so much to me, threw a towel over the computer, so it wouldn't call to me—picked up the dust cloth (I truly AM a woman of the cloth, y'see) and realized once again, that Love "covers a multitude of sins" and picks up an awful lot of junk!

And so, God revealed His plan to me, gently, via the telephone, the doorbell, household chores, the demands of others. And what was it all about? It was about being God's representative in the midst of daily living—and being about His business, by minding my own assigned busy-ness. It was His Presence, not so much in the milling crowd, but in the sweetness of solitude—or while wiping a counter top, scraping a broiler, scrubbing a stove, folding a sheet, cleaning a carrot, doubling a recipe, refinishing furniture, wallpapering, painting—He was, and still is, there to assist, comfort, remind, grant patience, give confidence, cheer, and lend companionship.

In short, it is nestling down into one of the tender maxims of Christianity, for someone much wiser than I stated that "the chief end of man is to glorify God and enjoy Him forever." There is only one way to enjoy Him forever—by learning to adore Him in the joyous NOW—for this moment—and the next—and the tumbling next—the sum total of all our moments being—forever!

The Prissy Little Princess

Once upon a nervous breakdown, a certain daughter of the King went fumblingly on her way. She had a tendency to fuss and fume over every circumstance she found herself in. She could be peevish about even unchangeable things like, for instance, the weather! And she was seldom satisfied. Even when she was thin, she thought she was fat. And though her castle was adequate, still she complained. She had a fine husband, a real prince of a guy; hardworking, thoughtful, and ambitious, too. But she complained about this, as well.

Now if the truth be known, our heroine had everything going for her. Why? Because she knew God. But she couldn't be satisfied here, either. She consistently whined around the castle that she "didn't feel loved." Well, I guess you could say that even her knowledge of God was very vague; still, our heroine had developed a pretty good habit of getting on her knees and talking with God. Granted, her prayers were rather puny and cockle-burred with many "Oh, give me's" and heavily scented with a lot of woeful "if only's" for you see, she'd come to believe that her happiness depended on her outward circumstances being a certain way. If she could just manipulate God and others around her to conform to her way of thinking, why of course, THEN she could be happy!

Little did she know that this attitude stemmed from a

strong desire to control.

Well, fortunately for our little princess, her Father the Almighty King overlooked this proneness to control, and looked more deeply into her heart. He knew that the deep longings of her heart had been planted there by His Spirit and all these other "waste products" would be burned up by the fire of Spirit once she granted Him control. So, the King wasn't as concerned as were the other subjects of this kingdom she was trying to set up for herself. For daily, you see, she made the other lives of the residents of her kingdom quite miserable. She made her husband, the handsome prince, feel most inadequate. She was constantly making demands of him that he couldn't fulfill. Her children were not happy either, because the Princess had been given the important responsibility of establishing a happy atmosphere in said castle and was not fulfilling her sacred duties in this realm.

But one day, our fretful little Princess was crying. She saw that her mental garden was completely overrun with nettles, briars, and weeds. The fruits of the Spirit she'd so hoped to harvest and bring before the King were being choked and strangled by so many negative thoughts. With great resolve, referred to as "an act of the will" she set about untangling the vines that had grown around the fruit trees. And as she worked, she suddenly stumbled upon something—Oh, see! She found the keys of the Kingdom! She was ecstatic as she fondled them! There they were in all their shimmering glory, just waiting to unlock the rusted chambers of her heart. The biggest and the heaviest key of them all was marked "acceptance." With great care and perseverance, she applied that key to her heart, but found it needed much coaxing as it hadn't been used for eons. But gloriously, it seemed to be the master key—the one that would make the others "fit."

As she hesitantly began to accept herself, with all her limitations and weaknesses, her abilities and uniqueness, she found it quite easy to accept her husband, just as he was—and wonder of wonders, she found that the very essence of yielding to the Christ within her meant accepting circumstances as they were and as having come directly from God's hand, fashioned in Love for the very shaping and molding of her life.

Now when she got up from her knees, she understood that if she really meant it when she prayed, "Lord, I give you my life, my heart,"—the way to prove it was to get up from her knees and accept all the circumstances as being meted out by a just and loving God, exactly perfect the way they were.

One of the other keys was tagged with "giving." She found out that "giving, expecting nothing in return" entitled her to a deeper abundance of love than she could ever have hoped for or imagined. She found out that nowhere had she ever been commanded to "feel" loved, but only commanded to give love—to sow love, because eventually, you reap what a huge harvest of whatever you have sown.

Well, needless to say, the discovery of these keys had a profound effect upon the Princess's little family. They all clapped their hands in glee, as love and joy began to fill up the castle. And as the writer of this little story and the clap-happy Princess are one and the same, I can honestly tell you that they all lived haphazardly together, right up until at least the penning of this story, continually "keyed-up" and ready for anything the King commanded!

Insights

To think there was a time in my life, many decades ago, when possibly the heaviest anxiety I had to endure was whether or not my seams were straight. Those were the carefree days of running boards, pompadours, unsplittable atoms, Glenn Miller and the traditional sprinkling of acne.

Now I am the mother of six, the wife of one, the sister of multitudes and the grandmother of twenty! I've always thought the most difficult thing I have done for the Lord was to raise those six children. And sometimes, I wonder if they really got "raised." I think "being propped up and supported while growing" would be more accurate.

Yes, I loved my children—and still do, amazingly. But after raising six, I wasn't certain I'd ever get all that excited about having grandchildren. Oh, I knew I would smile and coo over them as any mildly interested grandparent should.

But then, I discovered this tremendous secret—you see, although I am almost anatomically ignorant, I have scientifically made a discovery that has probably already changed the world, and no one knows it! It has something to do with a little internal appendage in a woman's midsection that no one knows anything about, for it can't be detected by an x-ray machine. It is shaped like a tightly closed rose-bud, that lies there dormant until—wonder of wonders—you catch sight of that very first grandchild!

The Joy of Six!

Then, the Love of God fans it into the sweetest aroma that seems to permeate your entire being, filling you with that most necessary substance called grandmotherliness. Then, as the days go by, and that little one begins to wrap you around its delightful, chubby little finger, you realize at last why you had children—and then tell those children, gleefully—so that you could have grandchildren. And they just grin and know that you don't really mean a word of it. But nonetheless they humor you, because—who knows—now maybe they, too, will have grandchildren someday!

But the entrance of each grandchild heralded in something so precious—and always so writable. Our little Kari Rene was the first to break the sound barrier on the Potterbaum shores. Because of her refusal to make her way down into the birth canal (she has always had a mind of her own) she was ushered into the world by Caesarean section. She was the first grandchild on both sides of the family, so her birth announcement had to special. Here it is:

"Twas the day before Easter when all through Mom's tummy,
Not a pain was found stirring in my poor tired Mummy.

The rubber gloves hung by the scalpel with care—Just in case Dr. Middleton needed them there.

And I, I was nestled in Mommy, in bed,
While visions of doctor bills raced through Dad's head.

So Mom in her IV's and Doc in green gown,
All settled back to see if I wouldn't "come down."

When out on the monitor my heart made such a clatter,
The nurses all ran to see what was the matter!

Quick as lightning it all happened—Dad's mind's in a whirl!
A Caesarean debt, and a shout, "It's a GIRL!"

Kari came into this world with big brown eyes and oddly shaped blood cells. In fact, her blood cells were shaped so oddly, her spleen kept gobbling them up, thinking they were intruders in the kingdom. When she was six weeks old, I mentioned to Jan that she seemed awfully pale. It seems the doctor agreed. It was a frightening number of days for all of us, until we found out that she had a hereditary disease called "Spherocytosis." She had to have blood transfusions every six weeks until her spleen was removed when she was four. I am grateful that all of these transfusions came about before the AIDS scare. But guess what? Her body had manufactured six extra little spleens to take care of the heavy load of gobbling required by the original spleen she was born with! What a miracle the human body is!

And now, lest I never get the chance to show off like this again, I want to share an invitation I created in the wee hours of the morning, when preparing for a grand shower to celebrate the coming of our little Maxwell!

Just gimme a drum roll and turn the page, please...!

The Joy of Six!

You are invited to a "Maxwell" House" coffee!
A flavorful way of saying
Welcome!
To
Maxwell David Fritz
Who is the "unique blend"
Of
David and Laurie Fritz

This "brew-ha" will be held on the grounds of Max's friend,
Juan Valdez (AKA Grandma Potterbaum)
on the rich slope of the mountainside at
1000 Dreamway

2:00 p.m.
Saturday
July 13th, 1996

It has been twelve years since Maxwell's
Mommy brewed a little life, so what
She had has been shared, shredded, stained or
rusted, and all of her
Diapers were GOOD TO THE LAST DROP!
At the current time she has itty-bitty things from 3 to 6 months, but as you know, boy just keep growing...and growing...and getting strong!

If something "goes on the Fritz" and you CAN'T make it, please
pour out
Your tale of woe to us by calling
(205) 555-2121
as Aunt Jan Engle will help filter these plans

EXPRESSO News flash! Baby Maxwell will not be coming in via the Stork, but with the help of God and a caring surgeon, who said that baby Maxwell should STEEP Until July 31st
And will become a fresh cup of joy, early that morning

Piercing Thoughts

Last night I ran a nail through my foot clean up to my kneecap so today I'm still fussing and pouting around about it. I was nursing the wound and just generally pampering my low threshold of pain when I decided to corrupt myself with some TV. I watched part of one of those insane situation comedies where Pop is an absolute dolt and Mom has all the brains, and realized that our children would come to accept this as an American way of life.

But the commercial was the killer! A slender gorgeous arm was seen pushing the miracle vacuum—with just the itsy-bitsy-est pressure from the right index finger with such ease that it almost pushed itself. I thought, "Yeah, they told me that pierced ears wouldn't hurt, too."

First of all, if her duties have been so carefree, then why didn't her arm look like a giant ham hock? If her life is so simple, how does she burn up any calories? Now I must admit I have this little callous on my own index finger that comes from pushing the button on the washer, the dryer, the dishwasher, the light switches, the air conditioner, the toaster, the mixer, the TV, the VCR, the garbage disposal, the garage door opener, the telephone, etc. But I still have to face the fact that our lives aren't simple. We live at a pace in this country that drains us emotionally—and so much of our bustle is unnecessary. When we stand before God, He isn't going to hold us accountable for manicured lawns or spotlessly clean homes. He will hold us accountable for those who stood before us with tears in their eyes. He will ask us how we responded to those who were hurting. He will know if what we did for others came from a motive of Love for Him, or just as a means of relieving feelings of guilt or needing to impress someone.

We will feel such loss when we realize we failed to love our neighbors as ourselves... and we will feel a keen sense of loss when we acknowledge that most of all, we failed to love ourselves.

Well, I really don't know what all of this has to do with our slender lass with the pushy fingertip. But I can give you a big tip! Take a few moments out of every day and check how you feel. Do you feel good and warm and loving? Great. You are in harmony, lovingly aligned with God. Do you feel resentful, angry or put-upon? Great—these are negative nudges that have come along to get your attention to make you know you are out of harmony—and it only requires a change of thought and a sprinkle of willingness to get back on the right track. The "switching" from down feeling to up feeling works like a muscle. The more you try it, the easier it becomes. And there is no right or wrong way to do it!

Examine your motives in the light of God's Love. Learn to spend time tapping the resource within. The God who lives there, and longs for fellowship with you sends you all those wonderful, sensitive messages to guide you on your way back to Him. Yet, we make something so simple so very difficult.

Oddly enough, just writing this chapter helped me to let go of some negative feelings. See how easy it is? And that sound you jest heard was my halo clattering to the floor.

Soap Opera Leads

I've often been asked why I didn't write Soap Operas. I don't know whether those comments came about because of the drama that seems to wind up at the same place I do... or could it be the complaining I've done down through the years?

Who knows. And who cares? Because I am doing much better now. Actually, I mentioned just yesterday, that it is a shame to know the curtain will soon be falling on the Last Act, when one is just getting the hang of living life the way it was meant to be lived.

However, I do tend to hear things that seem hard to believe and would certainly make good soap opera material. For instance, a phone call that went something like this:

"Char? This is Liz. Do you have a few minutes? Girlfriend, I need to talk. I've just made a discovery that has almost shattered me. As you know, Mom hasn't been given much time to live. Char, she pulled me down on the bed beside her and proceeded to tell me that my precious dad wasn't even my father! Good heavens! I'm a thirty-four-year-old woman and I'm shook to the core!"

"Liz, maybe it was just the delirious raving of a very sick woman—"

"No, Char—I checked with my two older sisters. They cried and went all to pieces, too, but they said they'd known for years, because I was born when they were teenagers...

Honestly! Oh, Char, it only makes me love Dad all the more... he's loved me as dearly as he has the others. I am so grateful to him! But he's obviously forgiven Mom many years ago so I'm not going to bring it up to him."

"That's good wisdom, Liz"

"But Char," she continued, "The other uncomfortable thing is she told me who my real father is and I know him!"

I gulped. Wow... makes me wonder if some things aren't better taken to the grave, and yet I know this isn't true. While watching the Oprah show yesterday, the subject was about dying, and wonderful touching things we can learn bout ourselves and others when the crisis strikes, and how this very crisis makes us open up to those we love in ways we may never have been able to, otherwise.

It becomes a time for earnest sharing and deep forgiving. The saddest thing of all is that many couples cannot open up to one another until the threat of parting by death becomes a reality.

Another interesting situation was shared with me many years ago. I had a friend whose sister had a somewhat similar story, but it was worked out differently in their various lives. For the sake of anonymity, I will call her sister Alice.

Alice had had one child, a boy, when she divorced her husband. Not too long after the divorce, she found herself pregnant by a man she had come to love. The lover was a married man who supported her for as long as he could during her pregnancy, but the guilt and shame became unbearable for him. He confessed the situation to his wife and begged her forgiveness. Once the initial shock had worn off, his wife did some careful thinking about the whole situation.

Once she felt certain that he didn't wish to end their marriage, nor did she as they had their own children to think about, she made a decree. She told him that they had the room—they would take Alice and her son into their home, and when the child was born, they would take the babe and raise it as their own.

Alice moved in with them when she was in her fifth month. This wonderful woman who befriended her became a good, gentle and loving friend. She taught her how to do canning and how to make preserves. She taught her so many things and was always kind to her little boy.

These people were not church-going people but they knew how to show God's love and to live the forgiveness that is so necessary to heal the wounds of the world. After the birth of the child, Alice left their home, and I am happy to tell you that she remarried her first husband and they lived happily, for many years, until his death. More forgiveness—more mercy shown. It isn't such a bad world, after all.

And there's more! Enter the dear adopted grandchildren!

Before Mark and Becky even got married, I'd heard them mention in passing, that "Yes, they wanted to have their own natural born children, but they also wanted to adopt some." But somehow I was too busy setting the table or something to take that in as anything serious enough to think about a second time.

Well, six years ago, I realized they were quite serious about this promise they'd made to one another. Mark and Becky had two natural born children, Michaela and Bradley, but because of very difficult deliveries, Becky was told not to have any more children. But you know how these mother-hearts can get—well, she began to have an earnest

The Joy of Six!

yearning for another child and wrote of it constantly in her prayer journal.

Adopting wasn't all that easy. As they already had two healthy children to lavish love on, the authorities didn't take them too seriously as they were more concerned with those who had no children. Becky was getting discouraged. But a neighbor of theirs, who had just adopted a precious little bi-racial boy, said "Becky, if you don't care what color of skin your baby has, the Catholic Charities will see that you get one much quicker!"

Well, it wasn't long before we were bouncing our wonderful baby Tyler on our knees! He is our beautiful little bi-racial boy, but when it comes to skin hues, thank God — we are all color blind! He was only 28 hours old when we got him, and that, quite unexpectedly, as it all happened so quickly! I had the joy of holding him for the first three hours he was in our family, as they had so much to do, setting up the nursery and all... but within a few days, a social worker called to say, "The birth mother wants to meet with you."

Becky tried to act calm until the appointment, but underneath she was dying a thousands deaths, as the birth mother still had the right to take that baby back at any time until all papers where legalized. Becky put a lot of thought into what a young teenager might enjoy. She prepared a basket of fun lotions, make-up, and CD's that uplift, decorated it beautifully, then wept over it, as she felt so much love for this young girl who had given her the gift of Tyler. She had also started a moving memorial to Tyler's homecoming by putting photos and many of the loving prayers she had prayed as she waited for his arrival, into a Memory Book.

The social worker's office was about two hours from

Mark and Becky's home. The whole family, who were used to laughter and fun banter, made the trip in somber silence, and very prayerfully, I might add. Upon arrival, the entire family was made comfortable in an office, and the birth mother and her father were introduced to them.

Becky said, "Mom, there are no words to describe the experience. After we'd spent almost two hours with these dear people, the little birth mother with tears running down her face, said, 'I am ready to sign the papers now. I just had to know what kind of people would be raising my baby. I had to know that you were more then just Sunday church goers. Your hearts are full of love and joy so I know you truly will raise him with a love for the Savior. I only wish— I only wish I could go home with you, too."

Becky explained that the birth mother's father, a very distinguished looking man, said, "I am terminally ill, and I cannot leave this world in peace knowing that she was facing life alone with this child. It is so comforting, knowing that he will be in your care." Becky said, "There was such an overwhelming feeling of Love, and an overpowering Presence of pure peace... it cannot be described, but it always brings tears to my eyes, just recalling the experience. We had taken two small teddy bears with us, exactly alike. We gave one to the birth mother, as a reminder of Tyler's love for her, and the other we promised we would keep for Tyler to remind him of her love for him."

It was sheer joy, watching Mark and his family love this little boy into toddler-hood. It appears that many were watching this family expressing love in an everyday kind of manner, as Becky had a cleaning lady who often brought her young teenage daughter with her. It wasn't unusual for the daughter to also include a certain friend, as helping with the Bed and Breakfast that Mark and Becky had at the time

The Joy of Six!

was so much fun!

One day, this "certain friend," a fifteen year old girl, approached Becky and asked if she could talk with her. When Becky dropped what she was doing so they could chat, this young girl broke into tears and fell into Becky's arms, sobbing. Dear Becky, very used to doing much counseling through their former work in Youth With a Mission (in fact, this is where Mark and Becky met one another!) allowed her to quiet down as she stroked her head for a few minutes.

Then the little lass spoke softly and said, "Becky—would you and Mark be willing to adopt my little three-month-old son? I would only adopt him out if you would be willing to take him...Becky"—more sobs—"I don't even know how to be a fifteen-year-old, much less a good mother! I now know I have to do what is best for him. I see you with Tyler—I see what a good daddy Mark is...Oh Becky, will you take him, please?"

So Mark and Becky took little Devin into their lives and hearts, quickly realizing that he, too, was to be a part of their family. A most harrowing situation came up when little Devin was six moths old, a situation so disturbing it felt like Mark and Becky were going through a loss by death, their grief was so intense. It looked as though the adoption would not happen.

But God intervened, and on Mark's birthday, the adoption was made legal in the courtroom of our county. Mark wanted us there, for it was a momentous moment for all, but the little birth mother and Devin's grandmother were sitting with us, and I could hardly bear their grief, although they kept assuring us that, "No, these are tears of happiness as well as sadness—please don't feel badly. We know this is best for him, and our hearts are so full of gratitude, that he will have a good home."

And so, all the nerve ends began to settle down into place once more. In Tyler's fourth year, Mark and Becky felt God was calling them back to Youth With a Mission (and I cannot say I was even surprised...I always had the feeling deep inside that they would go back to the mission field someday.)

They found a couple who loved cleaning, cooking, yard care, and people—it was just the combination needed to run a Bed and Breakfast efficiently, so off they went to the YWAM (Youth With a Mission) base in Nashville, leaving this couple to hold down the fort here on the home front.

About a year and a half into this new ministry, they got another call from Catholic Charities. Mark broke the news to me like this: "Hey mom! How are you? Uh, are you sitting down? I'm calling to tell you that we are just a bit pregnant. In fact, we are going to have TWINS in just a few weeks. (They had just been to my house and I knew Becky was still into a size 8, so my head was whirling...)

From a far distance, I heard myself squealing, "Mark? Twins? Are you both insane?" And I may have fallen off my chair, but Mark howling and cracking up on the speakerphone brought me back to reality and lots of deep breathing and the proverbial white-knuckling thing.

It seems that Tyler's birth mother, when she found out that she was going to have twins, knew she could not financially handle this, and asked the Charities to see if Mark and Becky would take them so they could be with Tyler. Of course Mark and Becky didn't refuse the offer—but the adoption was much more complicated as the twins were born in Ohio, and Mark and Becky were now residents of Tennessee.

So Becky and the children came back here to stay, as we

are much closer to Ohio than they were in Tennessee. What a fun month! Becky and I would pass in the hallway, and as we heard something crashing to the floor I would roll my eyes, and say, "People are more important than things!" and Becky would smile and say, "And nothing lasts forever, y'know..." and we would go to our assigned tasks. Well, one of us would make sure there were no injuries, first.

It meant many trips to Lima, Ohio where the twins were in the foster care of one of the dearest couples I'd ever met. The children couldn't be released from Ohio until papers were flown from Ohio, to Tennessee, to Indiana, back to Ohio, then... well, you get the picture. But what fond memories! Becky likened the twin's stay with the foster parents as "finishing up the womb time" as they'd been born prematurely, which is often the case with twins. We are so indebted to that dear couple and their helpful daughter and appreciated deeply the quiet serenity of their wonderful country home.

I would also like to add this footnote: If you have been adopted as a child, I can assure you that in almost every case, your adoption came about because of a parent loving you and wanting the very best for you. As I have witnessed all three of these adoptions I experienced the truth of that. It would feel much better on the inside of your wounded heart if you carried this picture, instead of the one that probably plagues you in the middle of long, lonely nights — tormenting pictures of abandonment, rejection, sadness. You would feel released into more joy if you would just flip the light on in your room, sit up in bed, and paint this new picture... one of love, caring and great concern for your welfare. It will feel so much better.

Recently I discovered that for over twenty years, a group called "Brickwall Survivors" (those who have not yet found birth parents, and those who were not well-received upon the finding) have been using a prayer that was taken from my second book, "Thanks Lord—I Needed That." They have adapted it to fit their own needs, and I feel so honored that they have chosen this prayer to ease the pain they bear when feelings of rejection take over. We are all where we are today, because of choices that our parents made! Yet, He promises us that "all things work together for good." Yes, even this.

Mall Maneuvers

A lady passed me in the mall one day, and realizing it was me, she turned back and after a brief greeting touched my arm and said, "Charlene—you know, you can get yourself into more things! I never saw anything like it!" She walked away shaking her head and I felt momentarily rebuffed! Inwardly, I was fuming...I thought whatever is she referring to?

And then, all by myself, I stood there in the mall and had a good laugh. My son had been married for not too many years to a girl named Sharleen. (during the years I was doing speaking engagements, I used to say, "You will never meet another with a name as unusual as mine" but little did I know...)

I howled because I finally figured out what this woman was referring to. Shortly after Shar and Larry were married, Shar ran a Junior Miss Pageant, opened a dress shop, ran a small newspaper and dabbled in real estate! No wonder my Mall friend thought I was too busy! And besides all of this, Shar and I have managed to get our UPS orders all tangled up, doctor's records confused, phone lines crossed—along with some banking bloopers thrown in.

About that same time, a woman stopped to chat—again in the mall—and she said, "Now Charlene. I want to know—in your books—did all those things really happen to you or did you make most of them up?"

I giggled and replied, "Even my zany imagination

couldn't whomp all that stuff up....why do you ask?"

She said, "Oh, I don't' know...it just seems like a person can't find something funny in everything that comes your way. Take the laundry, for instance. How could one ever find anything funny in that!"

So I remembered something I'd put in one my books. "Well, what with six kinds and all, our laundry got so big I finally gave it all to Good Will—then after they'd washed and ironed it, I bought it all back!" It's really strange, but it seems like a lot of people walk away from me shaking their heads! There can't be that many palsied people around.

And while on the subject of malls, I recall another incident. It happened during a really hot spell in July, when my husband owned the appliance store that was directly across the street from our home.

The fuses in the air conditioner at the store had blown, so when he came home for a coffee break, he put some money on the countertop and very nicely asked if I'd mind going down to K-Mart to buy some fuses.

Naturally, I said I'd go as I was very much aware of K-Mart's proximity to the Tastee Freeze, so who could refuse an offer like that? I went into the bathroom to powder my nose and make myself presentable. As I was about to leave, one of the teens stopped me and said, "Wait, Mom—before you go, check out the fruit punch I just made—does it taste sweet enough?"

I saw that it looked cool, refreshing, and very deep purple as he handed me the dripping mug, so I quickly slugged down most of it and assured him it was perfect, as I sailed out the door.

In K-Mart I found the fuses, finally, by accosting several floor clerks, who, I might add were extremely cheerful, considering the stifling heat. In fact, some of them were

The Joy of Six! 127

even kind of giddy, I thought, for they were even giggling. I made my way to the front of the store and waited in the long line for my turn to check out.

Even the checkout girl seemed to be in a wonderful mood, as she, too stifled a chuckle. I put the clammy fuses I'd been holding in my hands (for what seemed like a week) down on the counter. She rang it up, then laughingly said, "That will be $2.46, please."

But when I reached into my purse, I made the discovery that I'd left my billfold at home, where Gene had placed the money! But not to worry—I saw I had my checkbook, so I twittered, "Oops! Guess I'll have to write a check, alright?"

She nodded her assent, but somehow found it excruciatingly funny as she put her hand over her mouth, laughing hysterically. People were steadily lining up right behind me and I remember wondering if all the fuses in the city had gone out. I handed her the written check. She grinned even more, and chirped, "Thank you—and may I see your identification?"

Now, had there been any saintly shimmering about me at all, you can be sure it disappeared on the spot, as through gritted teeth I reminded her that "if I'd had identification, I'd have had my billfold with me, and would not have needed, therefore, to write the blasted check!"

I turned to the patrons waiting so patiently behind me, and saw that they all grinned in response, so I felt safe in setting this little darling straight! I cleared my throat, and cozied up to her by leaning on the counter. I said, "Look, dear. See the name here? Potterbaum's—the big store right down the street. We are neighbors—and the check is only for $2.46. Now, if it was a fifty dollar check, I'd say you could be concerned, but I'm good for this, so please find someone who can give me the permission to go, please?"

Well, within a few minutes I was out of the store, thinking what a lousy situation that happened to be...and with that, I reached up to adjust my rear-view mirror, only to gasp and come close to passing out! I had a ring of purple punch on my face that made me look like a smile-god-loves-you button, which, from my vantage point seemed to go from one ear to the other, with puddles in my dimples! (Needless to say, this became known as Mom's punch line.)

Gene groaned when he heard me tell the story. He said, "You told them what your name was and who you belonged to?" (Poor choice of words, I know—but he is from the Old School.)

Poor man. I have no idea why he has stuck around this long!

Moods

Just hearing the sound of that word "mooooods" ought to keep us from sinking into one. It sounds like a calf bawling for its mother. Or is it me, bawling for the Perfect Parent? And rightfully, I think that is what God is—our Perfect Parent. When I need mother comfort, I go to Him—when I need a Father's love, I go to Him. He is always so readily available, because, you see, He lives right here inside of me which makes Him closer than breathing. So, of course, wherever I go there I am—and so is He!

It is such a wonder to me that He can be so accessible considering He has to pump all our hearts, work our lungs like a bellows, sift through our kidneys, make that long journey from top to bottom (how many miles of intestines?) look after the outcome and rest our bodies, lubricate our joints, stash our memories in a file, storehouse our feelings, keep guardians on our footpaths, repair our damages, send nerve messages hither and yon so they get there at the right time, guide our intuition, keep all the electrons lit and the molecules dancing and the atoms whirling, all the while creating beautiful things for our eyes to see, fanning tantalizing things our way to be sniffed, and shooting dreams into our imaginations just for the fun of it! And besides, that, He has to fill all the heavens and the earth with His Being! Whew! All of this, for a little clod of dust that has perfected how to pout, rebel, ignore, whimper and whine, turn away from and resist this Goodness. What a wonder He is!

When Things Need To Be Ironed Out

Getting to the bottom of the ironing basket is, for most people, a milestone, a happening. For me, it is costly, for alas! I see that all the styles have changed! And a season or two gone by, as well!

Well, while working on wrinkles, and what could be thrown back into the dryer for another go-around, and what truly needed to be ironed out, I recalled a story I loved about a pastor friend of ours who ironed out a disturbing problem he had with one of his flock. It seems that Joe, one of his congregants, had this really frustrating habit of saying he would do something then never doing it, or promising to buy someone something and never following through. All of his promises were like so much fluff.

One day, our friend the pastor walked up to him and said, "Hi, Joe...say, that's a snazzy shirt. Where'd you get it?" momentarily forgetting the fellow's weakness.

"Oh, this?" responded Joe. "You really like it? Hey, I'll buy you one. Sure thing, I will," he beamed.

Our quick-witted friend parried with, "Fine, Joe. Meet me tomorrow, as soon as you get off work, and I'll just let you buy me one, and just to be sure you get the right size, I'll even go with you. Wow, I really like it...sure hope they have one left...see ya' after work, Joe!"

Later that night, the pastor called Joe's wife. He said, "Sue, I'm going to reimburse you for the cost of the shirt

Joe's going to buy me. I know you kids are strapped, but I feel like Joe needs to know the meaning of integrity. I don't think God wants us to go around saying we'll do things we have no intention of doing. Joe needs to know how expensive idle words can be. Will you be my accomplice in this? If it seems a bit deceptive, God will hold me responsible, not you."

She was elated. "It'll be an object lesson he'll never forget," she laughed.

Well, Joe bought him the shirt and Joe learned to "put his money where his mouth was."

But what about the rest of us? Have you ever had anyone say "Let me know if there is any way I can be of help," and then when you let them know you are in a bind, you make the discovery that those words were just hollow, trite and often said because it was the right thing to say?

But lessons like this cause you to watch what comes out of your own mouth. I recently read a book, The Four Agreements, that admonished us to be "impeccable with your word," and the author, Miguel Ruiz took it even a step beyond, by saying that we should also watch what we say about ourselves—TO our selves!

With my children, I have told them they always had the right to ask for what they might need, but we always had the right to refuse the request if it interfered with our plans. So, I only babysit when it works for me, and when I can do it without a shred of resentment—of course I always pinch-hit in emergencies...well, I don't pinch or hit babies, but you know what I mean.

Although we all more or less agree that words have great power, I want to stretch beyond that and throw you a curve... for I believe it is the attendant spirit behind the words that are spoken that makes the difference and generates the

Power! I believe we are coming into an age where children will not so much listen to the words we speak as they will listen to the spirit that stands behind the words that are spoken!

I remember a time when I came home to find that someone had made flour and water paste and gotten gobs of it on the carpet, and someone had been sawing something in the kitchen! It felt like there was massive clutter everywhere, and I began to reprimand the kids in a manner that landed somewhere between tight-lipped and explosive! They took it, but began to slink away like little shadows, feeling quite unloved, I am sure.

Then as I was angrily trying to clean up the mess and give them crabby directions as to what they were supposed to do, I hard Jamie, who was about seven at the time, mutter, "Wow, Mark. It doesn't even feel like home, does it?" And with that, my heart melted.

I held up my hand, and said, "Whoa there—hey you guys, Jamie is right. It doesn't feel like home, does it? Kids, you needed to be scolded, for what you did wasn't showing respect to this house, but I had no right to go at you like some ol' Meanie-Mom, did I...I shouldn't have yelled at you the way I did. I'm sorry."

Mark turned those tender blue eyes towards me, and said with a look of amazement, "Jeez, Mom—I think moms are supposed to yell, aren't they? All the other kids' moms do!"

Well, it was good to know I wasn't alone in the Land of Pick Up and Put away, after all. And so, as we started to pick up and put away, I was amazed how the energy had changed around us. The mood shifted from dejection to soft forgiveness in the space of a few hearty hugs. There truly is a softer, gentler way to live.

Last Day Mentality

Believe me when I tell you I am not a born housekeeper. No, I was "born" towards beds of ease, not beds to be changed; more toward dallying and dreaming, not rallying and cleaning. The Mary side of me wants to read luscious books, write to my heart's content, and space out by daydreaming all I wish, but one call from my mother-in-law and her imminent appearance can bring out the Martha in me slicker than jelly on a light switch!

I feel that creative people have a difficult time keeping up with what society requires for a home to be "acceptable." Now that I am further generationally removed from all that wonderful "kid clutter" I want to shout that the perfection of the home is not the first priority! The kids are!

Yet, I can identify with young mothers when they get discouraged. I remember the feeling of frustration, especially when I'd see Gene leave for the store, all togged out in suit and tie, clean-shaven and smelling good, while I faced cobwebs, candy wrappers and empty Coke cans. There were times when I had a cleaning lady, to better assure me some sanity, but there were also times when I didn't. At one of those times, I recall going into the boys' room and almost gagging.

You see, I am of the tail-end of the women who were wedged between "your children should be responsible for their own rooms" and the generation that believed "if a woman cleans the house, then she cleans the WHOLE house, and the critics be damned!" So I did a lot of fluctuating. In this particular week, I was queen of my domain, and the entire house was going to be cleaned, come hell or high water marks!

I found a deep resentment and anger surfacing! I felt put upon, taken advantage of, not respected and just every general downer feeling you can think of. As I was turning tumbled socks right side out while sand and grit flew all over, I was muttering and scowling as things crunched under my feet.

But suddenly, in the midst of all this fussing and fuming, I heard a gentle Voice say, "Charlene...be gentle. What if this was the last chance you had to do this for these children. Pretend that it is, and see what that feels like."

I went limp. I hugged the offensive stocking to my breast and tears rolled down my face as I sat on the still rumpled bed. What a change in perspective! Love flooded my soul, and everything I touched sang with the Love of God, after such an awakening. Because no one knows...it could be my last day. Or it could be the last for one of them. My heart was flooded with the importance of treating each day as though it would be the last. I mean, think about it...Our words would be so much kinder, our thoughts so much more forgiving; our intents would be guided by love and inclusiveness; our actions would be so much gentler...we'd truly wind up with the softer, gentler world I mentioned before. It only takes looking at things in a different light from a different frame of mind to bring this about. And—it takes practice! But it is so do-able.

That was a real turning point in my life. One I shall never forget.

Memories

See if this brings back any memories. The scenario ran something like this: Yawning, harassed, fighting-flu-bug mother realizes that alarm was set for the wrong time. Makes way gropingly to inner recesses of second story where various bodies are draped, snoring, gulping and snitzeling.

Mother says, testily: "We're late!" and gently smacks fanny end for emphasis. "Get a hustle on, and come on down and eat."

Sleeper: "Uh-hmmm. Be right down z-z-z-...ick, glump—right away –z-z-."

Mother with firmer whomp on snuggled-in fanny: "Hey! I mean it! Right now! Up and at 'em."

Mother makes way to kitchen, fumbles around getting breakfast while endeavoring to get cobwebs out of numb brain. With a pang, realizes that one particular body hasn't revived enough to sidle into niche at breakfast table.

Mother yells: "What IS the hold-up? What are you doing?"

From nether regions upstairs: "Ma, I can't find a shirt that fits—can't find one that will go with these pants—where is everything?

Mother in self-defense: "That's ridiculous! All the wash is done!"—Oops! The load with shirts—I'd meant to do that—hm-m-m. "You've plenty of shirts up there!"

(Mother makes dramatic strides up stairs with martyr-like sighs escaping from between clenched teeth) "See? You've a closet full!"

Downcast teenager: "Ma, look"—as he tries shirts on, exposing huge wrists, bulging biceps that can't be covered—growth too soon, too rapid for Mother to take in. Mother: "It can't be—I—well, that's no excuse. Put on a different pair of pants—you've shirts that will go with blue jeans—you can wear your cords another day."

Mother retreats in a huff, hearing son state, "I'm just a rotten kid I guess." (Author's note: Martyred mother not yet familiar enough with active listening to jump on the bandwagon. Correction: Mother aware of active listening and need for it, but too limp to know how to react. Correction: Mother too stubborn to react properly; finds that active screaming more suited to mood.)

Dejected and forlorn child enters kitchen. Silence reigns.

Mother responds, hostility melting, somewhat: "You'd better eat. You are late already. A few more minutes won't make that much difference."

Morose child: "I'm not hungry."

Repentant mother: "Honey, why do we do this to one another? I really do love you, y'know!"

Child, with touch of interest: "I don't know, Ma—maybe I could eat a bite," as he proceeds to devour breakfast.

Mother, who is now dying a thousand inward deaths, begins to purr: "Tell you what. I'll do my part if you'll do yours." (Weak response, I know, but mothers aren't perfect, after all.)

Child answers, while smearing peanut butter off finger onto adjoining kitchen stool: "What dya' mean?"

Mother, cringing inwardly while gently handing him a

napkin and gesturing toward neighboring kitchen stool: "I'll go through the drawers, clear out everything that is too small, and we'll go buy some new clothes. You start putting your things out at night, so we don't have this hassle in the mornings."

(Mother makes negative mental note: How many times in the past has such a suggestion worked? Only twice—with both daughters. Not only did they lay their clothes out—they started at four o'clock in the afternoon, put five combinations together, tried them all on. Left discarded ones in a heap and resorted to a ten thirty phone call—"Staci? Do you have something I can borrow to wear tomorrow? Oh good—My red blouse? With the fake patches? You want that? Okay—I'll trade with you as soon as we get to school.")

Mother deposits erring child at school. Child brightens as he sees peer group. Probably can't wait to tell them what a rotten mother he has.

Mother returns home. Calls school to explain why child is tardy. Pleasant voice says, "No need to explain. Your son told us he missed the bus."

Mother weeps quietly before the Lord. "Father, forgive me. I've blown it again. My son could have blamed me for not getting the shirts done, for not setting the alarm properly, for being such a grouch. But instead, he just said he missed the bus. Lord, I told him I loved him—but I didn't mention those three other little words, as in 'please forgive me.' I know that all things work together for good, so would you please allow something beautiful to come out of this little charade? Bridge the gap between what happened and what should have happened here this morning—between what was said, and what should have been said. Speak a special peace to his heart right now, Father. Thank you, Lord. Amen."

End of scenario? Hardly. For the present moments have a way of making their way into the future, leaving the memories of the past to hurt, crush, irritate, bless or heal. Would I seem extremely crude, if I told you that I think of God as my blessed Satellite Beam-catcher? I say the prayers to Him, and He beams the Love back to those for whom we pray, and because of their responding Love, they catch it...only sometimes, they don't even know it!

When the Birds and the Bees Made Their Entrance

We were all in the car coming home from church a number of years ago. I quietly announced, "I forgot to mention that I am having that mole removed from my upper lip so I won't be taking any speaking engagements this month."

Laurie was a very young teen at the time She asked, "How come?"

I said, "Because I think it would be most distracting to watch a lady speaker wearing a bobbing ecru Band-Aid that looked like a mustache."

She countered, "That's not what I mean. How come you are getting the mole removed?"

I put my finger on the mole and screwed up my mouth all funny. "Because sometimes it feels like it's pulling, or could be growing or puckering, or something."

"Huh," she snorted. "How would you like to be me and have these ugly old pimples pulling all over your face? Maybe I should go with you!"

I looked at her beautiful flawless face and knew that either I needed to get my bifocals checked or she needed to wash her bathroom mirror.

Meanwhile, two more adolescents bearing our name stopped their argueing from the backseat as to who was Mom's favorite, which one always had to do the most work, and who always got his own way the most—just long

The Joy of Six!

enough to chime in with, "Yeah, Mom. How would you like to have an ugly old face like hers?"

Gene, always the model of placidity, took my hand and assured me that some day they would grow up and then we'd all be friends again, and wouldn't that be nice? And he also assured me that he'd always thought that mole was a beauty mark, but if it bothered me, then yes, it should go.

Shortly after we arrived home, the boys came to me and said, "Mom, since it is so rainy Mick just called to see if we could show some movies in our basement. He said he'd bring his projector. Could you run us down to the Library to get some films?" (This was waaaay before videos was even a word!)

Shrewdly, I bargained with them. "Tell you what. Yes, I'll run you to the Library, and yes, you can show films down there if you will clean up your side of the basement. And just to show you that I'm all heart, I'll clean up my side, too. Deal?"

And not being overly meticulous they finished their side of the basement before I did. As I swooshed fuzz-balls hither and yon, and generally stirred up a lot of silt, I glanced over to their side of the basement and saw that they were being enraptured with statistics about the Titanic. I couldn't help feeling all warm and motherly to think that they were being so resourceful by finding such a constructive way to spend their rainy Saturday afternoon.

Wanting to reward them for being so agreeable I went upstairs to bake some cookies. A bit later, just after Micky had hurried out of the house Mark came into the kitchen with a rather troubled look on his face. Jamie came in quietly behind him.

Mark spoke first, a bit hesitantly—"Mom, what's a stag movie?"

"Why do you ask, dear?" I managed to squeeze the words through tightly drawn lips as I poured half a bottle of vanilla into the cookie dough.

"Micky started to show one. At least that's what he said it was called. But as soon as I saw what it was going to be, I jumped in front of the projector and flung my arms all around—like this." He leaped spread-eagled into the air.

Jamie looked thoughtful. "Yeah, thanks Mark. I pro'bly would have watched it, if you hadn't done that."

Weakly, I parroted, "Yeah, thanks Mark," as my knuckles turned white from clutching the countertop. Needless to say, a phone call to Micky's mother was in order as well as a little chat with my boys.

Another nudge in this direction happened a few days later when my next door neighbor, Toni Decker, swung in, laden down with one of her twins under each arm. (We called them the Double Deckers.) She placed a large children's book on the table, borrowed a cup of sugar and sailed out, saying, "Here, take a look at this. I got it from my pediatrician as the other kids were starting to ask some questions, so when I found your kids peeking at it, I didn't want you to think we were showing them pornographic literature! Let me know what you think of it, and then do what you want to about your kids reading it!" She left with a trail of dogs, babies and sugar.

Well, it was a book of cartoon sketches about the birds and the bees, and hilariously well-done, I might add. However, I was a bit put out, as the sketches looked very much like my shape, and I felt a bit miffed, as the book was intended to make you giggle while putting you at ease regarding the material. So Much for my being a sex symbol.

But the time had come. We did what we could with the material we had and blushed our way through to some kind of understanding of the facts at hand, which, as a matter of fact, was my take on the situation; I told them if God had asked me about this sex thing, I'd have told Him that I'd always felt a nice handshake would have been much more lady-like for said experience, but this resulted in gales of laughter, as said children kept coming up with THAT scenario, such as—

"Oh, great Mom! Now I know why everyone always wants a 'handyman' around the house!"

And another parried with, "Guess that's why they call us guys Handsome, right?"

Another, while rolling in laughter on the floor, smirked. "Yeah, and everyone would start wearing gloves to cover up their private parts—and every hangnail would become a social disease!"

And someone shouted, "That's nothing—we'd be playing patty cake instead of spin the bottle! And Dr. Ruth would be—a Palm Reader!"

Grinning, I simpered, "Animals! All you men are – animals! And after all, it was just a thought—not shared by many, I'm sure!"

"Well, certainly not by me!" grinned my dear husband.

Testings

Just after my eldest son turned 21 and was still living at home, he nonchalantly walked into my kitchen and placed a partially filled can of beer in our refrigerator. It was almost as if I could hear the Lord saying, "Testing—one—two—three—testing." And I got the message.

I went on about my business as though he'd been doing this for years. We were not accustomed to having alcoholic beverages in our refrigerator, as this was in our Baptist days—nor do we have it there now, as we never developed a taste for it.

After this can sat there for a week and a half I decided to pitch it, for not even the finest beer could hold up in anyone's refrigerator against the fumes of a garlicky casserole and a soggy box of turtle food. As I was pouring the remainder of the beer down the sink, the can slipped from my fingers and fell smack-dab into the center of the garbage disposal! It fit so perfectly, that not even the slimmest, daintiest fingers would ever reach, grip, clutch, or throttle this strategically placed missle.

I thought if I wet the end of a rubber-tipped dart, just maybe I could ease the disturbing nuisance out of the disposal. I knew I had seen a dart recently, but after peeking through all my fern fronds and breaking two nails while scrunching through couch cushions, I gave it up.

About this time, the doorbell rang. A lovely young woman stood there, and she said, almost apologetically, "Oh, I know this is most unusual, but Dr. McGill, your neighbor"—she was pointing across the street and down the block a few houses—"said he knew you'd be more than willing to talk to me, and I'm so desperate. Can you take a few minutes to talk?

"Of course I can. Come in. But how did you find me? How did you know where I lived?"

"Well, I forgot to get your address from Dr. McGill, but I remembered him saying you had quite a few children, so when I saw the gym shoe on the roof, I somehow thought--"

"Say no more!" I laughed. "What else did Dr. McGill say?"

By then I was giggling heartily, and I explained to her that Dr. McGill and I had never met, but felt we knew each other so well from the books that each of us had written, we decided to keep it that way. We corresponded through letters, and found it more satisfying to just be heart friends, rather than neighbors.

We had moved into the kitchen by now, and after I made her comfortable, I continued with the problem at hand—or not quite at hand—the beer container in the garbage disposal. She watched with interest as I struggled, but still disbelieving, she said, "But you are neighbors! You've both written books! Why haven't you met?"

As I was bent over the sink, I said, "Honey, he has much wealth and prestige, and his mission field is the Country Club set. Me? I have a gym shoe on my roof, crab grass, and a beer can stuck in my disposal. Our common bond is Christ, and we both feel some day God will set up our first meeting—quite by accident."

And finally, in a burst of sheer genius, I cried, "Scotch tape! A big, fat, sticky bunch of Scotch tape will do the trick!" With that, I reached into a drawer, made a thick wad and very carefully extracted the can and pitched it into the trash.

It wasn't long until I discovered why the good doctor had sent her my way. She had adopted some pretty bad attitudes toward her husband, and the marriage was headed for trouble. I could see that they had forgotten that they were both on the same side and had ceased being partners, but were competitors. I gently encouraged her to paraphrase a well known idiom, by encouraging her to ask "not what her husband could do for her, but what could she do for her husband." And wrapped it all up with one of Gene's maxims—"If you treat your husband like a king, he will treat you like a queen!"

As we chatted, I was throwing a casserole together for our dinner. When I reached into the small tin of dry mustard, I felt something go "Clunk." And there sitting in my measuring spoon, was a yellow dusted puzzle piece that had been missing for some time.

We burst out laughing. I gave it all up as a bad try and poured us some coffee. Then, as she was leaving, she pointed upward and said, "Say, if you ever get a beer can stuck in your disposal again, there is the rubber-tipped dart you were looking for!"

I glanced up and sure enough, big as life—there was the end of a rubber-tipped dart sticking out of the overhead light fixture! I grinned and exclaimed, "Hey—I knew I had filed it away somewhere—just couldn't remember where!"

Game Players

I think it is fun that we still have so many little games we play. We have the 'dress up and look neat for the sake of others' game, and frankly, I quite like that one. We have the one that is 'don't say what you really think, or you might offend someone.' H-mmmm. Well it has its place, I suppose. But the one game that people seem to enjoy most is the 'can you top this?' game. This one I really like because it keeps the conversation moving along, and in this day and age, that is almost a lost art. You know how it goes—someone tells you something, and then you say, "Oh, yes—something similar happened to me like that , just the other day" and before you know it, you have a go at the game, yourself.

Well, recently I heard of someone who had left a book on top of their car and never did find it as it must have flown off to heaven knows where—and it reminded me of an adventure we had so many years ago. I hadn't thought of the incident for years, and it bears telling here because miracles are always "in" and as far as I am concerned, this was truly a miracle! There have been people who have hinted that we were born under a lucky sign, or something—in fact, one time a woman asked me what sign I was "born under" and I told Gene that I never knew what to say when people asked me this. He thought for a moment, and then said, "Why not just tell them the sign said Elkhart General Hospital?

But here is my miracle-draped story:

We lived across the street from our store, called "Potterbaum's Appliance City." This was before malls, Sam's, Wal-Mart, Circuit City, or any of the other biggies that dot all horizons now. The store was open until eight, and Gene had just called to tell me that he was going to make a late delivery. I was due to have Jamie at the time and didn't rest well anyhow, so I opted to scrub the kitchen floor while the troops were nestled in for the night and the "runway" was clear of little feet and debris.

I was sloshing around in the soapy water and having a generally good time, secretly wondering if a little slip in the suds might not shorten my waiting period when Gene appeared through the back door in a visibly shaken condition.

"Char, you can't imagine what I just did. As I was about to get into the truck to make the delivery, I saw that the merchandise wasn't secure enough, so before I got into the truck I foolishly put the bank bag with all the day's receipts in it on top of the bed of the truck. I retied the rope of the refrigerator I had to deliver, then got back into the truck and took off—I forgot all about the bag! I didn't remember it until I left the customer's house. It really made me sick, but I know that it's done and over with and God only knows where that bag is now. I retraced my route but it's pitch black out there, and I couldn't see a thing."

I wanted to be the understanding wife and make all the right comforting sounds, but I, too, was dismayed when I realized that the bank bag contained probably close to three thousand dollars in checks, cash and contract sales. Most of that money was needed to meet the store overhead and debts we had to pay for merchandise. We did our best to release it into God's hands and went to bed with heavy hearts. The next morning's message at church was uplifting.

The Joy of Six! 149

It was centered on trusting God with our treasures and giving our all to Him. I couldn't help thinking Boy, have we ever! A whole bag full! We felt there must be someone out there who needed it worse than we did or Gene would have found it when he went out so early that very morning to scour the route he'd traveled the night before.

As we drove home, our hearts were very refreshed and we couldn't help giggling with the kids about the sights we were seeing. You, see, this was only a few weeks after the Palm Sunday tornado that had ripped through our area and debris from the storm was still scattered all over. The sight that sent them into gales of laughter was a shredded bra hanging from a tree—they were too young to realize how the debris reminded us of the grief, the loss of life others experienced—and the additional hopelessness of ever finding the bank bag because of the debris. We were on the same road Gene had taken the night before but he had given up on finding anything.

We were singing together when suddenly Gene slammed on the brakes and, after a careful glance backwards, began to back up the car.

"Gene, I am eager to get to the hospital, but whiplash isn't what I had in mind—and have you lost yours? What are you doing?"

"I don't know for sure, but I'll tell you in a minute" he said as he got from the car and headed for a ditch. He backtracked for a few feet walking gingerly through broken bottles, cans, scattered clothing, busted limbs and tangles of weeds—and picked up the missing bank bag! I could hardly believe my eyes!

Needless to say, it was a time of real rejoicing in the car! Gene got into the car and gave us all hugs and said, "We were all singing and I felt so good. The loss didn't seem so tragic at that point, but I saw a glint of sun hit just the metal tip end of the zipper—that was all I saw, but I thought it was worth taking a closer look—and I'm sure glad I did! Wow, I am so grateful!"

And what a great thing for my children to witness! The goodness of God happening before their very eyes!

Networking

I read in one of Wayne Dyer's books something to the effect that networking would be the wave of the future. I think he was referring to how the Universe dishes up unusual happenings as people search for answers, and oftentimes just the right ones show up at exactly the moment you need them. I know my very own sister has been used so many times by God, on my behalf, and she wasn't even aware of it. Sometimes, while doing research for a book, she would run across something and say, "Sis, is this anything you could use?" And it wasn't unusual to have it wind up being one of my most arresting chapters.

But there is another kind of networking I want to mention because it is so close to my heart. I remember years ago, being at a financial seminar and in the midst of something the teacher was saying, he stopped and said, "By the way, I want to throw this in—I want to tell you that network marketing is a very good thing. If you can find five people who will find five other people and if they all do exactly as you do—you will all become very wealthy." That was his take on the matter, and quite frankly, that has always been my impression as well. I can't say that I have really hankered after wealth, but being financially free has always appealed to me, and you will have to agree that network marketing has created probably more millionaires than possibly any other venture I have ever heard of!

Please understand that I am not trying to sell you something. I just have always thought it was an incredible way to free people up so they could do what they love to do—it could bring in great income for mothers who wanted to be stay-at-home moms; it seemed like a way for people to make a great income and still pursue their life's dream; it always seemed like the means of being free to travel while your business was working for you while you were away.

I marveled at a man in our church who was able to amass a whoppin' 7500 people in his downline in just two-and-a half years! Once, over coffee, I asked him how he managed this. He said, "Well, I am not certain I'd do it this way if I had it all to do over again, because it wasn't exactly 'duplicatable'. However, I needed to have income coming in quickly, so I told an Amish man I knew, that if he could get several Amish men together, I would be giving away a horse as a door prize! That worked like magic, as he got around 200 assembled, and over 100 signed up that night. The scheme worked so well, I did the same thing six months later, with the same results. The Amish people go for homeopathics, and put more emphasis on staying well as opposed to focusing on sickness. I just happened to be there at the right time, I guess."

One of the reasons I have always felt that network marketing was open to us as a way to help one another comes from a well known story in the Bible. Now, dear ones, I am not saying I had a revelation here—but I am saying that I saw a picture, an outlaying of a program that represented network marketing to me—and it was laid out by Jesus Himself. It has to do with the feeding of the five thousand, and much of my thinking came from the fact that when the disciples came to Jesus because they were concerned about the people who would grow faint on the

The Joy of Six! 153

journey home if they didn't have some kind of sustenance, his quick reply was—"You feed them!" And due to their stammering and hem-hawing, he showed them how it could be done.

First he prayed, then He took things that were healthy and broke them up into small pieces, instructed the people to sit in units, then had the disciples distribute the bounty among the people and they were all satisfied. They even had gobs left over!

Well, it's just a picture. But it spoke volumes to me.

How I Found Lennie

Or maybe this should be titled "the Goodness of God" as this is when I realized how truly and divinely loved I was. The first book I wrote was If You See Lennie and the whole title was to have been If You See Lennie, Tell Her I love Her, but the publishers nixed that. The book came out in 1974, which is about the time they halted horse-drawn-carriage milk deliveries, if you want to know how long ago it was!

I was a total nobody.

There was no reason under the sun why anyone would be moved to read a book I had written. I'd been invisible as a child, so my married brothers and sister had only just discovered me and not having adjusted to that yet, I then had to deal with being flung into the public arena.

I got the word that my book had been accepted at Whitaker's on the day we were meeting with friends at the church, so naturally I was eager to share with my pastor. Gene happened to be standing with me when I bubbled out the news to him. The pastor looked dumb-founded for a moment, then looked at Gene and said, "I didn't think she could pull it off." Gene said, "I didn't, either." So much for support and celebration. Actually, I wanted to knock their heads together, but I was too happy to follow through. But the next comment by the pastor really bothered me. He looked at me and said, "I seriously doubt it has any convicting power, however." It was his kind way of saying "it won't affect anyone's life much," and I wouldn't have been surprised if he'd have reached over to pat my head. But I am pleased to tell you that he was wrong, as I got mail from all over the world, stating that "their hearts had been touched" or "I came to Christ when I read your book" and lots of other heart-warming, encouraging words.

(And one of the neatest, most recent discoveries happened just a few days ago. A lady in her eighties called to say, "Charlene, this is kind of embarrassing to even bring up, but I have had your book about Lennie sitting here in the bookshelf right by my bed for over thirty years now, and I never read it until just the other day. It really made an impact on me, and I feel it will be just right for one of my relatives having a marriage problem right now. Would you be willing to counsel her?")

Writing a book can be a rather heady experience but I'm glad I opted to do it. The books opened doors to speaking engagements, and they can be an even headier experience, for the further you travel to speak—the greater an expert you become! But I love the writing best. That first book was a book of letters that I wrote to Lennie, as she was a wonderful neighbor, but when she moved we truly lost touch with each other. She moved out of state, and I kept having babies—too much to keep up with, I suppose, so the correspondence thing wasn't happening. But when I knew I had to write all the things down that were happening to us I didn't have the foggiest idea as how to start—but I remembered that I had always—and still do—loved writing letters! So it seemed a reasonable way for a novice to begin. As I pondered who I should write to, I decided it would have to be someone I could talk with freely, and someone who would make me laugh and Lennie fit that description, perfectly. It seemed logical to me, that if the book became published, then I just might find her someday, through the book.

I made the mistake of telling someone that I was writing this book of letters to a neighbor I couldn't find, which was pretty much par for the course for something I might do, but he, dear soul, said, "Letters! They're not 'in'—that won't work."

I thought a moment, and then muttered, "Well, I was just reading some letters this morning that were written two thousand years ago, and they are still on the bestseller list." I have found out since, that everyone has an opinion and it is much better to keep your creations a bit under wraps until you are ready to launch them—seems wiser, somehow.

As I went on my merry way speaking around the country, many wanted to know what I thought Lennie's reactions would be when she became aware of the book. I explained that her first reaction would be one of wonderment, but her second take would be—"Yeah, that would be something Charlene would do—just to save the postage!"

But this is what happened when Lennie 'found' the book: As I traveled around, I looked audiences over, always wondering if she might show up. Many years went by, and I still hoped. Then, one Sunday I found someone trying to get my attention at church. She said, "Hi, I'm Marion, and I met you at Lennie's house many years ago—do you recall?"

As I studied her face and ran a check through the memorabilia clogging up my brain, I said, "Yes, I remember meeting you!"

Naturally, the conversation got around to Lennie and the book and she asked if Lennie was aware of the book. I told her that no, I didn't think so, but that I hadn't given

The Joy of Six! 157

up on finding her through the book. She looked thoughtful for a moment, then she said, "You know, I think I have her current address and phone number—would you like to have it?"

"Oh, yes, I really would," I sweetly lied. Actually, I was devastated, because I had wanted so very much to find her through one of my books. That very next Wednesday, we were having coffee with some friends after church when the phone rang. Gene answered it, then pulled me aside and said, "Char—I think it is one of your book fans," as he handed me the phone.

I heard a voice say, "Is this really my Charlene Potterbaum?"

Sensing that yes, this might be a fan, I sucked my tummy in, straightened my dress and pulled up the sultriest voice I could muster as I simpered, "Yes, it is."

Then she let out a whoop, and said, "Charlene! This is your Lennie—as in the book?" What a reunion we had! It was as though there had never been any years between us as we laughed and cried together.

I said, "Lennie—how did this happen? Did Marion call you?" and she said, "Marion who?"

"I met her at your home many years ago—just Marion... I don't know her last name—did she get in touch with you?"

"No, I've been trying to tell you—I found your book at the Piggly Wiggly Super Market—on the bottom shelf!" (I thought thanks, Lord—I needed that! Which happens to be the title of my second book.) She expounded further by adding, "I almost didn't buy it, because—well, I don't know—guess I couldn't believe that any one I knew personally could ever write a book! But with a name like Potterbaum—there aren't too many around, so I bought it anyhow. Then, when I got home and started reading, I knew it had to be you as I read, then when you mentioned your first book 'Lennie'—I threw the book up in the air, and screamed at my husband, "Les, quick—come here—I'm a book!"

We laughed and giggled our way through about forty minutes of nonsense, as I recall, made arrangements to meet in Erie where she resided at that time, then we said goodbye. Dazed, I went back to my hubby and my poor deserted friends. Gene had explained to them that someone at church had mentioned that she had a current phone number for Lennie, so that must be what this was all about. My company was very forgiving about being neglected, because they knew how much I hoped to connect with Lennie someday and they seemed rather pleased to be privy to the whole thing. Everyone started talking at once when I joined them for coffee again. Just as I was explaining to them that No, the gal I met at church had nothing to do with this reunion, and that Lennie had found me in a supermarket—the phone rang.

A cheery voice said, "Charlene, this is Marion—we met at church last Sunday? Hey, I had to do some sleuthing, but I finally found Lennie's address."

But I laughingly stopped her and squealed, "Marion! You are never going to believe this, but I just talked to her! She gave me her phone number and address, so I am all set! Thank you so much for following through with what you said you'd do, as most people don't do that—but can you imagine how excited I am about finding her through one of my books?" We said goodbye, and again, I went to my houseful of friends.

This time I was very quiet, and before long, tears were trickling down my face. Quietly, I said, "You know, if that phone call from Marion had come three days from now, I wouldn't have thought so much about it—but to have it come only fifteen minutes after talking to Lennie—I feel kind of overwhelmed with His love right now, because He respected my little-girl need to find her through a book enough to let it happen before Marion made that call—how awesome."

I share this with you, because so many have asked about this. Also, I love recalling His love to me and His ways of showing it. There are some days when I read through this current book, and I think "Blah—yuk. Who would ever care to read this—yet, there are other days when I read through it and think, hey—this is pretty good. I shared this with my friend, and she said, "Charlene, that's okay—because some days I really love my husband—but some days I don't like him at all, so it must be quite normal."

The Re-enactment, Jr. Style

When I share things verbally, I pay attention to the reactions of people as a way of testing whether or not the incidents should be included in this book. Two really hip great-nephews, Chauncey and Taylor, kept saying "cool" and "no kidding!" as I told them about the time we had returned from a trip to Gettysburg, many years ago. Mark was eleven and Jamie was almost nine. The night we arrived home, I forewarned the little darlings that I intended to spend most of the next day in bed, as I had contracted a really severe sinus infection and had no intention of functioning normally. I gave a quick-run down of what they could do and not do, and one of the specifics was to "keep the neighborhood kids and any fringe friends outside and away from my pantry."

The next day was a beautiful day and I groaned, because I hated to waste it in bed. However the "ague and I" were stuck with each other, so I pulled the shades shut and listened to the happy sounds coming from beneath my bedroom window. It seemed to be some kind of planning session, as I heard Jamie shouting, "Okay, you guys go home and you have to be dressed in either blue or gray when you come back, so we will know which side you are on."

I thought, Well, they took this trip to Gettysburg quite seriously. I was glad I'd taken the time to glue a red stripe down Jamie's navy blue pants before the trip and had taken the ears off of a Mouseketeers cap and covered it with matching navy material to make a kepi, or I knew they'd be storming the fort for substitutes. Mark wasn't quite as fussy. He was just happy to organize the whole thing.

The other sounds I noticed seemed harmless enough, as a cousin had shown them how to take a pop can, add a bit of lighter fluid in the bottom and put a tennis ball in the top, and you'd have quite an effective cannon sound to contribute. I felt they were wise enough, under Mark's supervision, to keep anything bad from happening.

I drifted off to sleep for awhile, but always conscious of a happy buzz going on somewhere down on the lawn. I was so grateful they had heeded my pleas for solitude, as there seemed to be no squabbling—just noises that felt like organizational tones to me.

It wasn't long until I felt an urge to eat something, so I made my way down to the main floor. As I yawned my way into the family room where we had a big picture window, I stopped dead in my tracks! I couldn't believe the panorama before my eyes! Prior to our going to Gettysburg, Mark had fashioned a cannon of sorts out of plywood, and he had spray painted it black. Today, one of the "grays" had thought of attaching an old pair of my pantyhose to it as a giant slingshot while a cartridge bearer was refueling the sling from a piled up stash of little green apples off the tree in the back!

The "blues," not wanting to be out-maneuvered, were using a giant empty spool that had once contained telephone wire and had another pair of my pantyhose geared for action, with a pile of buckeyes ready for the volley of exchanges. Out in the fringes of the yard, several lackeys were stationed to give the "boom" effect from the tennis ball-shod pop cans, when the cannon bearers gave them the high-sign. During my nap, they had all banded together to literally weave a hospital tent out of huge squares of unprinted newspaper someone had given them. A well-drawn red-crayoned cross adorned the top of this 'tent,' and just as I had stepped to the window, the battle had begun in full force.

Careening through the yard at a pretty good pace—considering their burden—came the medics, bearing a 'blue' with what appeared to be the whole bottle of my catsup dripping from his chest. I laughed until I almost cried, until I realized they had used one of my good dining room table leaves as a stretcher! They quickly placed him in this hospital tent, and at a signal when the 'boom' shot through the air, the said dying patient kicked for all he was worth, and of course, the tent flew all over my yard—as well as several in close proximity.

Yes, I stood there at the window, and I laughed, and cried, and praised God for the wonderful gift of imagination and ingenuity those kids were displaying—and I thanked him for the wonderful gift of memory, for that scene can never be taken from me, or from them as they recall that fun day. Many years later, Jamie wrote a tender song called "My back Yard" and the words nostalgically say "I see all the places, where all my friends hung out" but most of all, it speaks of this tender memory they all share. Whenever this was played at clubs throughout the area, by the second verse, a hush would come over the audience and one by one, the cigarette lighters would flip on and often, there were tears in the eyes, as people remembered their own special memories of long ago.

There is a verse in the Bible that says "a child shall be known by his doings." Later in life, Jamie became an actual Civil War re-enactor and did many "living history" re-enactments, including Gettysburg. Not only that, but he made the decision to have a Civil War wedding! I am sad to say that the marriage didn't last as long as it took me to make all the male uniforms. I was a bit apprehensive about attaching anything that smacked of 'civil war' to any word linked with marriage in the first place! Bad enough to know that a 'civil war' might ensue later without implying it right from the start.

There were so many other fun things that happened in that neighborhood. Toni, our next door neighbor, had four kids, and she was great about organizing parades and fairs for charities. We combined our two yards and turned the kid's imaginations loose, then did what was feasible and manageable from our end. Granted, our yards weren't the most manicured. I think there still might be some foxholes in that back yard from that war fiasco. And sadly, all those children are now grown. The fun whoops and noise that kids make are missing, now.

But those noises were most rampant when Mark and Jamie had a rock and roll band called "NRG" (I got into serious trouble if I failed to pronounce that as 'Energy). An affluent neighbor down the street did his best to get a petition going to keep them from practicing in our garage. The petition wasn't too successful, however, as one neighbor said, "Hey, my kids are having a ball over there—count me out." Another one said, "Are you kidding? At our age, we love seeing all that life over there," and another said, "Hey, they are using drums that my company makes—no way will I sign it!"

Jamie finally made his way to Nashville, to fulfill his dream of making his living through music, and Mark went off to Youth With a Mission to become a missionary and later, a staff member, where he met his terrific little wife,

Becky. Recently, Jamie came "home" to play several gigs here in town, and there were those former "warriors" from the backyard—some are dentists, firefighters, graphic artists, designers...but still little boys inside. They loved his "sound" he has developed for the many "Blues" venues who seek him out in Nashville. It is so stirring to recall these memories, and see that, truly, our lives are like a "tale that is written."

Those Illusive Tomato Plants

Many years ago, just after we had moved into our current residence, I pulled into the garage and as I stepped out of the car, I noticed a flat of tomato plants I hadn't noticed before. I remember groaning as I wasn't into gardening at that time and didn't have a clue as to where I would plant them, thinking some well-meaning friend had dropped them by...someone who didn't want to plant them any more than I did! It was really late, so I made my way to my bedroom, thinking that in the morning, or some day thereafter, I might put a few in front of the privacy fence, then I'd give the rest away.

I completely forgot about them the next morning as I rolled into the duties of that day. About mid-morning, Earl, our former next door neighbor and minister of one of the local Methodist churches, came jogging down our lane, and when I saw him I met him out front with a big glass of water to cheer him on his way. He stopped to chat a moment, and while chatting, he mentioned something about his garden, and that reminded me of the flat in the garage.

"Oh, Earl—someone left me a flat of tomato plants, and I really don't want that many—do you want some?"

"Sure," he said. "What kind are they?"

"I don't know—take a look!" and when I looked for the flat, it was gone! Suddenly, it dawned on me! Those weren't tomato plants at all! Then I blanched—then I cried.

"Oh Earl—one of my kids—they could get into so much trouble...I wonder who—And Earl said, "Oh Charlene—is there anything I can do?"

"No—I'll pull myself together in a minute." Then I started laughing, hysterically.

"Uh, Char, are you okay?" he asked.

"Can you believe it? I was going to plant some out there by the fence—and I was going to give some to a preacher! Not to the plumber, or the garbage man—but to a minister!"

Every one of the kids pleaded innocent, and I never did get to the bottom of those mysterious plants. One of the kids felt a friend had found access to our garage, knowing he'd have probably gotten killed had he taken them to his own home. I can't think of too many manuals that prepare mothers for things like this. But I do find people looking the fence over warily as they admire my garden.

One time, Larry had been doing some yard work for some friends so while burning leaves, he noticed some suspicious little plants nearby. (In case you are wondering, these little plants grow quite well in our part of the Midwest. I have even heard it rumored that the government planted fields of hemp here in our area for the making of rope during the war. Seeds do go through the air, you know. At least that is the young people's story and they are sticking to it.) He told me he plucked the plants and threw them on the fire. He said "That neighborhood will be grinning from ear to ear for the next week, at least..."

Making Points

I am convinced that people are sick to death of half-truths, masks, cover-ups and shallowness. The human heart of today that succumbs so easily to heart disease is also the same heart that longs for sharing, transparency, and integrity and that will search anywhere, go to any lengths, to find fulfillment—but mostly in all the wrong places.

Several years ago, I received this letter from a young housewife in Texas. She said, "I was raised in a Christian home but left God (had I ever really found Him?) as a teenager. Things went from bad to worse after I married and I eventually ended up on the verge of losing my husband, baby boy, and the respect of my very respectable parents. Why? Because of the age-old quest of looking for "love" and "fulfillment" everywhere except from the only true source of those two things.

"Well, apparently some of my 'Churchianity' stuck because one day I found my self standing in front of a Christian book stand in a Piggly Wiggly Supermarket praying. 'God if you're up there and you really care about me, you'd better lead me to a book that will lead me back to you 'cause it's almost too late.'"

I will take a moment here to express the extreme pleasure it gives me to say that He led her to one of my former books, and that yes, it did restore her faith, but not because of me, and not because God was "up there" but because the God Who lived within her resonated with the words I had written for it was His Spirit that prompted me to write them. The Spirit always goes looking for the Spirit!

PoChing said it so succinctly when we were talking about this very book you are holding. I was sharing a discussion I'd had with Gene and our son Mark when he was visiting here recently. I had mentioned to them that I'd soon be finished with this book, and then I was going to fling caution to the winds, and self-publish on the Internet.

Gene quietly said, "But no one will be able to find you." And Mark—dear Mark—said, "And Mom, I hate to tell you this—but the only ones who carry these Palm Pilots like I have in my hand are businessmen. They (ahem) won't be exactly interested in your type of book."

At the time, I couldn't help thinking so much for support from the home front! However, I have grown enough to know that Jesus was right-on when he mentioned that "a prophet is not without honor, save in his own country," so I wasn't too surprised by their reaction. I didn't go into any of the details, how one could just push a button and order from reputable book stores and have a book in front of them in less than a week. That still wouldn't explain my profound belief in God's ability to move upon people's hearts to "find" my book.

So, I ran all of this by my mentor, PoChing. "PoChing, don't you feel it is possible for God to move on people's hearts to read what I have written?

He studied the possibility in his mind for a moment, then with great enthusiasm, which is a scholarly way of saying "being filled with God," he exclaimed, "Oh, yes Chah-lene! The Buddha always find—the Buddha!"

I was not in the least offended, for I knew exactly what he meant. It was his way of saying "the Christ will always find the Christ" and I did a big thumb's up as I whispered, "Yesssss!"

PoChing and I have talked about this at great length. He has said, "Chah-lene, a true Buddhist does not bow down to some idol. He loves that which fills heaven and all earth, and we both love 'dis Spirit Who live in all—He just not as fussy about what He be called as people's tink. To love this won'nerful Creator is important ting—mos' important ting of all. Waste too much energy on not so important tings. God always looking to find expressions of Himself. If what you write speak of Him in true way—He will lead people to it. Ummmm, yes. This very true."

I have always been a firm believer that you cannot sink the Word of God any more deeply into the heart of another than that Word has sunk into your own. If your God experience has been shallow, so will that be, which comes from your mouth regarding Him. Have you ever had the experience of listening to a speaker, but the words seemed to be whirling over your head and never settling into your heart? Yet, I am sure you have been literally under the spell of other speakers where the very heart of God seems to reside in everything they say! This is a working premise for the difference between a shallow experience and "deep calling unto deep."

One of the points I want to make while rambling here as we share honestly, is this: That our hearts are starving for real and transparent relationships, but the fear and pain that is involved in establishing these relationships is so painful we take an easier route by reading about other relationships first, hoping we will find a quicker, more palatable remedy. I'm just as bad off as you are, because I can be more honest with you as I sit here before this computer, than I can be with my own family over the dinner table. But again, you don't interrupt as much as they do, either.

I can honestly say I am cash-register honest but still have not mastered the skills of being emotionally honest. It is a spiritual problem, so it needs to be solved on a spiritual level, but not on the same level where it was created. I have to "rise above" the fear that forms and move into a larger place. Why should doing one of the most important things in our lives be so difficult? Yet, I see so many people struggling with this issue. I think the real culprit could be "judgment." I have heard women say, "about the time I share a feeling, my husband finds a reason why I shouldn't feel it, how silly it is to feel that way, and then he starts laying the 'shoulds' on me. It's just simpler to be still and not make waves." So, many remain in the shadows and comfort a broken heart through food, drugs or other addictions.

However I am pleased to see that there is a younger generation coming up with a greater willingness to express feelings. Chauncey, my great-nephew, wrote a loving little word of encouragement to his friend, Kate, when she felt so stressed, not so long ago. Now picture this—Chauncey, typical football material for this year's season, and Kate, his pretty friend who had the moxie to look lovely in her prom dress while wearing comfortable sneakers underneath for comfort! This generation is coming up with more sense than we have had down through the ages, and they refuse to let the dictates of fashion control their lives. Here is Chauncey's stress reliever for Kate:

> Busy?
> All of my accomplishments are not for me
> but for you—
> My Eagle rank—
> My education and my goals.

You have aided many to find God, it's true.
Your holy duty now keeps you busy
But don't get stressed, sad, or mad, or blue—
Just keep on working
For I have a future to share with you.
Be patient—stress now? Happiness later!
Now you have a trillion things to do—
Someday with my help this won't be true.
You are my inspiration—I want to be God's gift to you.

****

We Come to the End of a Very Good Beginning

Writing this last chapter is very much like cutting the umbilical cord to a new birthing. When that life-line of cord is cut, it foretells the ending of one segment and a reaching to the next phase. A releasing, a letting go—yet, one of great joy, I hope. I think I have finally worked out why I wrote this book. I wanted to leave something that would live on after me, but it is even more than that. Many times I have started a letter to my children, as I didn't want to die with so many things left unsaid, but found those letters never got finished—or were grabbed up by the most current rash of grandchildren to be used as paper airplanes or snowflakes on the Christmas tree.

But just as no one should "die with their music still in them" (as so beautifully written by Wayne Dyer)—neither should one die with their wisdom still in them. I know that my parents did the best they knew how to do. I know that all that we endured together was perfect for bringing me to where I am today—but I must add this one thing. I never heard one word of wisdom coming from their mouths! Please know that I am not faulting them. They lived in an era when relating and deep sharing weren't touted. They spent a lot of time thinking, but never shared what they were thinking. The one thing I can remember my mother saying that would come even close, was the comment she made while in the nursing home when she was feeling so weak. She said, "Ohhhh, girls—It ain't the dyin' that's so bad—it's the gettin' ready to!"

Even in that nursing home, my sister and I learned something of great value. Pitifully, my mother would say, "Oh how did this ever happen?" and realistically we replied, "Mom it happened to you one day at a time and you have kept at it for eighty-six years." There is greater import in that than I realized, for all of us are practicing—daily—for what we shall be towards the end. If much of your day is spent in grousing and complaining, then rest assured—that is how you will end your days. If your days are spent in learning the sacred art of loving and forgiving, then your end will be gentle and blessed. It just depends in what direction you choose. But Mom was very incoherent at times and could become very verbal so it was necessary that whoever they put in the room with her could put up with her verbosity. I am not sure I was quite prepared for their choice. I shuddered when I saw her roommate Polly for the first time. She was ugly, lean and totally "out of it." She spent all of her time in the locked prison of her body going through arm and hand gyrations from her over-sized highchair that somehow gave you the impression that she was weaving or spinning. Consequently, we referred to her as "the spinner" instead of her given name, Polly.

On Thanksgiving Day my sister and I went together to visit Mom, this being her first holiday apart from us. Because of Mom's senility and misery, she seemed rather demanding. We responded to her "move my pillow—rub my back—get me water—scratch my nose" commands in love.

Our backs were starting to ache as we hovered over her, and once, while straightening out a kink in mine, I said, "Lauraine! That sound—what is it? I think it's the spinner—and I think she's crying."

Lauraine responded, "No, it couldn't be—I don't think she's capable of tears" but she moved as quickly as I did to Polly's side, almost fearfully, as the nurses had warned us to stay away from her as she had a tendency to get you in a vise-like grip and it would take the nurses to get her to release us.

But the hurting sound in those tears and whimpering and the obedience in our step caused something to happen. As we stepped from Mom's bed to her chair, a rush of unconditional love washed through our hearts for this unlovable wretch. I put my arms around her and Lauraine began to pat her arm as we asked her forgiveness for not seeing her as a real person. She couldn't answer a word as she hadn't spoken an intelligible word in years but she seemed to respond and wanted to look deeply into our eyes with and indescribable hunger for love and affection. I cuddled her head in my arms and began to pray, asking God to speak to her deep within her spirit, assuring her of our love and concern now that we realized she could even comprehend our presence.

Lauraine and I were both crying softly with her and feeling the Presence of the Lord as we gave a drink of cold water to this, surely, the very "least of the brethren." After we'd patted and loved her for some time, she released her hold on us, looked longingly into our eyes again, then clearly and distinctly whispered, "Than-nk you-u-u."

We were nearly beside ourselves with joy, and she had stopped crying. It became an even greater day of Thanksgiving for us when we heard that one grateful utterance. Lauraine and I looked deeply at each other, quietly wondering what shape we will be in when later years become a reality for us. We realized how really short life is and how important it is to allow God to fill each moment with His own pulsating, life-giving energy—the same energy that raised Christ from the dead. But are we aware that this same power is ours?

Now, as I wind this up, I am reminded of the dear ol' pastor who, when asked what his favorite verse was, smiled and said, "My favorite verse is—'and it came to pass'" Bewildered, the questioner asked, "And why would that be?" To which the old saint chuckled—"Cuz, praise God, it didn't come to stay!" and I haven't come to stay, either.

I want to wrap these memoirs in something soft and comforting, much like the proverbial swaddling clothes, so I have chosen a sweet, nostalgic bit of writing done by Melanie Moore. It is my way of keeping my word to her, as I had promised many years ago that I would try to get this published. It seems like a most fitting way to end this book, and an excellent way to keep that promise.

Relax into the mood she sets and enjoy the ambiance of her childhood retreat, The Nursery—written by Melanie Moore, of Texas.

The Nursery

Some of my fondest childhood memories take me back to a place I call the Nursery. The Nursery was located in Waco, not far from the Baylor University campus. It was situated on a large corner lot at 1215 Baylor Street. The property served as a location for Robin's Patio and Garden Center, my grandparent's business. However, there was also a house on the site, and I lived there with my family from the time I was four years old until I was six.

My grandparents, who I called Mamaw and Papaw, purchased the house on Baylor Street for Granny and Grandaddy, Mamaw's elderly parents. Because Granny had health problems and was bedridden, Grandaddy could no longer care for her alone. My mom and dad, along with my younger sister and me, moved in to help out. The house was an old white Victorian style house with a wraparound porch and gingerbread trim. I remember the ever present smells of pine cleaner and lemon oil in the house. Carpet had been laid on top of the oak floor, but it still made a pleasant creaking sound when I walked across a certain board. There were several huge windows in the living room, and I enjoyed standing here when the weather kept me from playing out side. I had a great view of the viaduct and could watch the traffic come and go.

The grounds of the nursery were beautiful, thanks to Mamaw's expertise with plants. There was lush, green grass that carpeted the yard, and nothing felt better on my bare, little feet. Bright flower beds lined the front and sides of the houses as well as the fence line by the street. I got into trouble more times than I care to remember because I couldn't resist the temptation to pick the fuzzy stemmed Gerber daisies.

In the middle of the yard stood a large wisteria bush with fragrant grape-like clusters of purple-blue flowers. It was the perfect place for my sister and me to enjoy a peanut butter sandwich picnic on a sunny afternoon. If it was a particularly hot day, we were sometimes allowed to splash around in the little cement pond near the front gate. It had a fountain with a lady spilling water out of a basket. I can remember exactly how it felt to catch the gushing water with my tongue. In the side yard there was a graceful crepe myrtle tree with dark pink blooms. It had smooth, paper-like bark that was great fun to peel off.

Very near the crepe myrtle tree was Granddaddy's strawberry patch. He always let me help him tend to the patch, even though I was much better at eating the ripe, sweet berries than picking the weeds. Just behind the strawberry patch and in front of the greenhouse was a cluster of large pecan trees. Those trees shaded the whole area, and the largest of them supported my tire swing. Towards the back of the property was the greenhouse, and the dirt-house was right beside it. The greenhouse was a long building made of fiberglass that contained row after row of every plant and flower imaginable. My favorite part of the greenhouse was the foggers. The foggers were very similar to the sprinklers in today's supermarket produce sections. I absolutely loved to stand under the plant shelves and get kissed by the fine, cool spray of water.

The dirt-house was an entirely different experience. It

was the building where Mamaw mixed soil and potted new plants. The dirt-house was dark, damp, and just plain scary. My Aunt Robin, who is only six years my elder, didn't help matters by telling me that the Ghost of Bloody Terror lived there. If I didn't do what she told me to do, the dreaded monster would surely come get me.

Our neighbors on Baylor Street were also a big part of my world. The Cantos, an older Mexican couple, lived directly across the street. They were very friendly people who spoke with heavy accents. I visited them often. Next to the Cantos lived a family with a chubby, dark-haired girl who was about my age. She could never pronounce my name correctly. Despite my repeated attempts to teach her, she always called me Lelalie. This frustrated me so that I finally bit her. As a direct result of that ordeal, I received a spanking I never forgot.

Next to the little chubby girl lived a man who couldn't hear or talk. He was a kind man with a constant, wonderful smile. I believed that my Aunt Robin was insulting him when she said he was deaf and dumb, and it made me angry. The pink house right next door to the nursery was home to the doughnut lady. When Mrs. Baird's Bread truck came around, she always purchased an ample supply of powdered doughnuts. The doughnut lady frequently shared them with us kids.

I suppose change is inevitable, and our life at the nursery was no exception. Grandaddy had a fatal heart attack while he was thrashing pecans. Not long after that, Granny passed away in her sleep, and her suffering came to an end. My daddy had just gotten a job with United Parcel Service in Temple, so my family moved to Bruceville in order to make the commute easier. Leaving behind the people, house, and yard was a sad experience for me.

The Joy of Six!

About a year after we moved away from the nursery, my Papaw passed away. Mamaw could not handle the business alone, so it was closed shortly after Papaw died. The house was then rented out for many years. The last family to rent the house did a lot of damage, and they finally even stopped paying the rent. Mamaw was forced to evict them. However, after years of neglect and abuse, the house was in a terrible state of repair. Mamaw decided to sell the place and Aunt Robin and her husband turned out to be the buyers. They purchased the property for a storage unit business, so the house had to be torn down.

The last time I saw the old house was just before it was demolished. Because vagrants had broken into the house, it was in even worse shape than the last tenants had left it. Windows were broken out and the carpet was badly stained. Instead of pine cleaner and lemon oil, the smells that assaulted my nose were mildew and urine. The once lovely yard was little more than a dusty weed patch. This drabness was accentuated by the absence of the beautiful flower beds. The only bright spot left was the wonderful old crepe myrtle tree. I walked over and peeled a bit of the smooth bark from the trunk. Across the street stood new condominiums. The little pink house was still next door, but the doughnut lady was long gone. It looked empty and lonely. There was little to remind me of the beautiful place in my memories.

When I last visited the property on Baylor Street, it was treeless. The only thing standing was the new, freshly painted storage building. It had a large green and gold sign advertising Bear Storage. Although the landmarks from my childhood are gone from the Nursery, I can still call up those happy times in my memory.

I even got to keep a souvenir of the wonderful old house.

My husband and I were able to recover and restore the original oak flooring from the house. After much sanding, finishing, sealing and hard work, the flooring is now in the upstairs bedroom of our home. Every time I walk across a certain squeaky board, I smile and think happy thoughts of the Nursery.

*****

Another wonderful word of thanks to you, dear Melanie. As you all walk across these pages, I pray that an occasional "squeaky board" comes up for you. I have a Diary written by a great-aunt back in the 1880's. As much as I love it, I find my heart yearning to know something of what she felt—or thought, as I wanted so much to feel her soul, but as I have mentioned before—it just wasn't done that much back then. Here, you will sense that I have poured out my being to you. I am comfortable with that. I hope you are, too.

By the way of closing I want to bring a paragraph to you that I just read, written by J.D. Freeman:

"Many times when we write about what makes us spiritual, we forget that joy has to be very near the top of the list. I pray that what I write and say and do will help people. When I help people to laugh, or at least to smile, I am helping them to live. We don't have to be helped to weep—most of us find reason enough for weeping. What we have to do is continue to grow and unfold more and more human happiness—and more and more humanness toward ourselves and others. A sense of humor helps us to do this."

I pray that what I have written here will help you to become more aware. I pray that you will be more conscious of the choices you make and of the thoughts you think. But most of all, that you will laugh as you go on your way—not only to the proverbial bank, but as you go to your homes, your schools, your in-laws, your jobs—and that the smile you wear will come from a deep place inside of you. May the Universe be a friendlier, happier place because you and I have met one another, here in these pages. God bless you all, and to all—a good buy! (Well, this is reasonably priced, you know!")

www.ingramcontent.com/pod-product-compliance
Lightning Source LLC
Chambersburg PA
CBHW051756040426
42446CB00007B/397